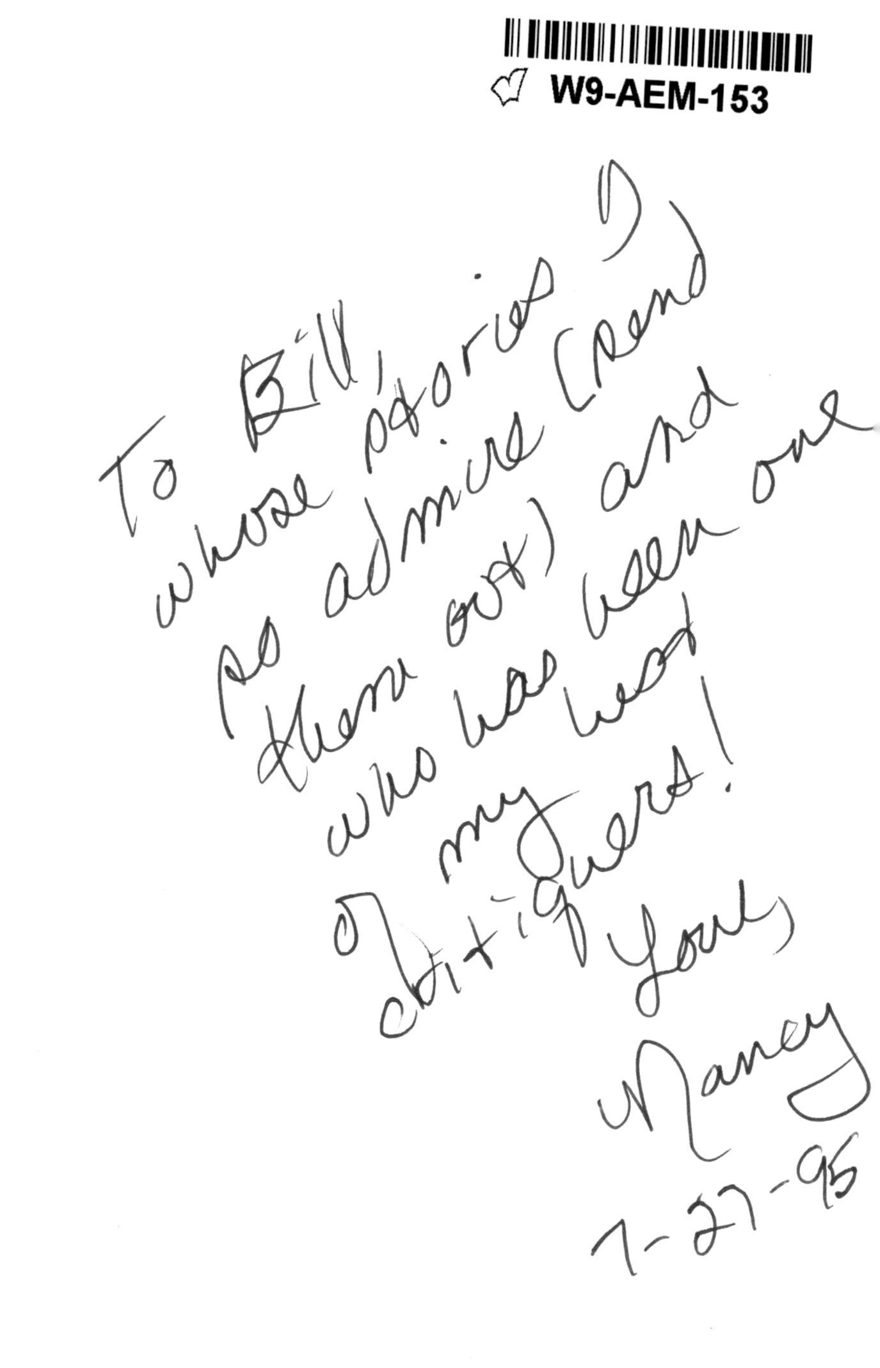
To Bill,
whose stories I
so admire (read
them out) and
who has been one
of my best
critiquers!
Love,
Nancy
7-27-95

Variations on the Ordinary

A Woman's Reader

Nancy J. Henderson, Mary Ann Wehler,
Aline Soules, Susan Knoppow, Pearl Kastran Ahnen,
Gerry Tamm, Sandy Gerling, Vivian DeGain, Nancy Ryan

Editor: Margo LaGattuta

Plain View Press
P. O. 33311
Austin, TX 78764
512-441-2452

ISBN: 0-911051-81-3
Library of Congress Number: 95-069500

For extraordinary women everywhere . . .

Cover design by Sandy Gerling.

Acknowledgments

The authors wish to acknowledge prior publication of the following pieces which appear in this book: *"Surfacing,"* **Embracing the Fall,** © 1994 Margo LaGattuta, Plain View Press; *"Somewhere in Spain,"* **Resourceful Woman,** Edited by Julie Winklepleck & Shawn Brennan, © 1994 Visible Ink Press, reprinted with permission of Gale Research Inc., Nancy J. Henderson; *"Not Fair,"* **Encore,** Mary Ann Wehler; *"Dream Catcher,"* **Nostalgia,** *Mary Ann Wehler; "On Easter, My 90-Year-Old Mother Wondered, Why Didn't You Go to Church?,"* **The Heartlands Today,** Volume 3, 1993, Mary Ann Wehler; *"Father's Last Night,"* **Graffiti Rag**, Mary Ann Wehler; *"Let's Just Go On,"* ***Heart Songs,*** Poetry Society of Michigan, ©1995, Aline Soules; *"Deep Black Pine and Paper Birch,"* **The MacGuffin,** Susan Knoppow; *"Making Babies"* and *"Barbie Clothes,"* **Resourceful Woman,** Edited by Julie Winklepleck & Shawn Brennan, © 1994 Visible Ink Press, Reprinted with permission of Gale Research Inc., Susan Knoppow; *"Arsenal of Democracy,"* **Northern Spies,** 1992, Pearl Ahnen; *"Dr. YiaYia,"* **Sun Dog,** 1990, Pearl Ahnen; *"Swing Shift at Dodge Main,"* **Northern Spies**, 1995, Pearl Ahnen; *"Detroit's Best Coney Island," "A Promise," "The Gypsy,"* **Northern Spies**, Pearl Ahnen; *"Nickel a Hug,"* **Kaleidoscope,** Pearl Ahnen; *"At Gramma's House,"* **Heart Songs,** Poetry Society of America, © 1995 Gerry Tamm; *"Remodeling the Chelsea,"* **Peninsula Poets**, Gerry Tamm; *"Morning Coffee,"* **The Lake Holds Its Breath,** © 1994, Gerry Tamm; *"Skating on Spice,"* **The Highland Voice**, Nancy Ryan.

Cover Art

Cathy Heno-Suffel is a celebrated Texas artist known for her unique collage paintings. The cover of **Variations on the Ordinary** is a 48" x 60" collage titled "*Strong and Beautiful Women*," which was inspired by Cathy's belief in the power of women networking. The original, in the private collection of Leslie Ann Williams, includes oil on canvas, acrylic on canvas, and different printmaking techniques. Cathy works with a variety of 100% rag, acid-free, handmade and mould made papers. The paper is soaked in water and embossed, using intaglio plates she has created. This gives the finished piece a highly-textured, three-dimensional look. The paper is then painted with different oil solutions to attain vibrant, unusual color combinations. The embossed, painted paper is hand-torn in different shapes and adhered onto a painted canvas. Cathy lives in Houston and has shown her work in galleries and exhibitions throughout the country.

Photos by Rick Ballantyne.

Contents

FOREWORD

Margo LaGattuta

A woman with a pen and a bit of courage is a dangerous thing. She might begin to weave her story with the same potent energy she uses to weave the chaotic elements of her life into a kind of order. She might begin to see the microwave or a loaf of rising bread dough as a metaphor for her experience. She might decide to allow the inner echoes of her heart room on the page, allow the extraordinary thoughts she carries around in her purse to be heard above the din and clamor of an ordinary day. *Variations on the Ordinary* is a collection of writing from nine such women. All published writers, they were selected for their strength of content and craft. Over the course of ten months, we met in my studio to collaborate. They brought poems, stories and essays, and we all put our minds together to build a tribute to women's experience. Sometimes it was difficult, as so many things in life want to take precedence over a dedication to art, but no one gave up. Rising to the occasion became an overriding theme, as we honed and chiseled our words. Each voice is unique and original, yet the common threads are woven together in a collaborative whole that is larger than the sum of its parts. There is something of every woman's experience to be found in this book. I want to thank Susan Bright, publisher of Plain View Press in Austin, Texas, for offering me this opportunity to select manuscripts and edit the anthology. Her dedication to feminist publishing, social change and personal freedom has been an inspiration. I want to thank the nine writers: Nancy, Mary Ann, Aline, Susan, Pearl, Gerry, Sandy, Vivian and

Nancy, for reminding me of the power of shared experience. They have shown me that the ordinary, seen through their eyes, becomes extraordinary, the plain becomes the magical, and the experience of being a woman in our everyday world is transformed through language and metaphor into a personal mythology. **Variations on the Ordinary** is a first book for each of them, and I am proud to introduce them to you with this poem:

Surfacing

A woman in the kitchen
begins turning into a canoe.
The tide comes in, and she,
buoyant from holding her own

in the turbulence of wild waves,
begins to float miraculously
up, above the toaster and micro-
wave oven. Small 3x5 cards with
recipes for braised lamb shanks

with oregano and feta, or home
smoked chicken salad, swim
around her, doing the lean breast
stroke, begging her to surrender.

Like a tropical sweet potato
she's waited years for this.
Brushing the crushed pineapple
from her hair, she grows oars

and, as if guided by an
inspired flounder, makes her way
effortlessly through the lace
of kitchen gadgets promising life.

She's spent years soaked
up in her life, like a ziti
with marinara sauce, and now,
now with this simple gesture,

this frivolous escape from
the frequent shoppers' day old
baked goods bargain table,
she floats, unbreaded and free

above it all, higher
than a nacho grande,
more delicate than mahi mahi
with lime and papaya salsa,

surfacing with her own dilled life,
a battered canoe that won't tip.
Her curved resilience built in,
she's creating herself from scratch.

—*Margo LaGattuta*

Yet the Mustangs Keep on Coming

Nancy J. Henderson

I experience the act of writing as a process that leads me to create meaning. As William Stafford said, "It is like two rivers that blend." The rivers of my introspection and my spirituality flow together to form my creativity.

I have read that the discipline of the writer is to learn to be still and listen. Taking time to contemplate or meditate on my own awareness allows me to pay attention and listen for possible subjects, ideas, stories, or philosophies.

As I try to take a lonely shot at finding some meaning in the universe, I am often perched on a canyon ledge or sitting under a one-hundred-year-old fir, or sometimes just gazing out my living room window. Watching the colors change in the sky, or on the side of the mountain, I paint them with a pen, with words that rise out of dreams. And there always seem to be too few.

Dreaming Wild Mustangs

Wild mustangs come galloping up
a vertical cliff, sheer and wide.
The canyon stretches out before me.
I am on a ledge with a camera.
I want to shoot a picture of the steer . . .
one lone steer is hurtling through
the canyon with the horses . . . antlers
wide as my arms. That is the picture
I want . . . the lone desolate antlers
framed in a red canyon. This is art . . .
the one lonely shot at meaning . . .
the one lonely thought
that no one else has had . . .

and yet the mustangs keep on coming.

Turquoise Power

Lying there waiting for me,
just a feather made of silver,
a drop of turquoise for color,
on a silver chain. When I am
in need of comfort, I wear it
so small, lacing my breastbone
with power; light and flat,
sounding like a rattlesnake
as it rolls on its chain.
Turquoise brings power
to women, the Navajo hold.
Theirs is a power like prayer,
silent, still, linked in faith.
It lives beneath the banks
of our daily grind for rent,
our automotive ride through life,
and waits till our comfort
has run out. Then it slides into
the breastbone like a snake, unafraid.

Giving It To You

As always, I want to tell you everything . . . about the mountains that are dotted with tall saguaro, fence posts with no fences, the dirt that is almost sand, and the holes that tunnel into prairie dog mansions beneath my feet.

I want you to see it as I see it. Climbing up a road that seems to end in the sky, I can't take my eyes off the naked rocks and the petrified cacti that store water in their skin, amazed at the aged splendor I can see.

I make this landscape sound like a woman, exotic in her nudity, her wrinkles, pores exposed, and her sunlight-shriveled skin. Take a look for yourself. She is only human.

A Shifting Inside

She's feeling it again. It's a lean, a weight, that pushes against her like a big cat against her leg, only it pushes all of her. It's soft like that, humming inside, wet nose, blunt claws that gently knead at her heart. Sometimes she sits with it and lets it roam around her mind — what if? What if? She tries to let it become concrete, find the reality in this yearning. Just how would it feel to pull up her roots, be all alone in a far away state where nobody knows her, she knows nobody? She's done it before. She knows what it's like. But that was before. This is now. She's older now. The risk-taker is not as strong in her. Her strength comes more from the familiar.

But still, it's there. It won't go away. This longing to be near her wilderness. A wilderness that grows inside her, but has little chance to thrive, surrounded by the concrete. If only she could live in the abstract and the details weren't important. Then she would go. The lean would be more like a wind that would surely blow her in the right direction. She would be the scent of change, riding into her own.

One Way To Leave

It started when I knew the distance between us would never close, like the banks of a river never meet. I knew the water between us was too wide. I knew you would not admit the water existed.

I stayed on one bank watching you sun yourself with assumptions, getting tan with the stories you held to be true. I reached, I reached, with stories of my own, and I tried to build a bridge over the river. The bridge never quite touched, it was too heavy with my weight. I dove into the water.

Soon I began to float with ease around the boulders, between mossy logs, away from the banks that contained me. I floated on out to the ocean, slowly, away from your reasonable shore. On out to my own sea with the wind as my guide, and found you could not follow.

Somewhere in Spain

Somewhere on the coast of Spain
I awake in the night
to a storm blowing heavily
off of the Mediterranean.
The third floor balcony furniture
shakes and turns like
the rain that hits it.
I get out of bed in fear
that it will hit the glass,
crouch behind the wall of the room.
The aged motel darkens
as the power goes out.
No one knows where I am.
Alone, my language can't help me.

This is where I am
when you are angry.

Denial

It's a risky affair
to wake a man from sleep.
Music will sometimes do it.
Alarms only shock
and swerve the mind
into sudden rousing.

A sleeping man
finds his bed consoling
no matter how lumpy or hard.

Pull the blankets off
and he will only burrow deeper,
seeking another dream
to replace the one he's in.

Coax softly,
his eyes might open briefly,
then close again . . .
many times . . .
before daybreak.

Spark

Outside my front door a firefly falls
through the dusk. I am caught
in the air with it, a spark gone haywire,
like the way we spar when we disagree,
the way we hurt when we try to make sense;
or is it only a passion we let run away with us? Here
descending the stairs of my house in July,
I catch the firefly in a jar, hold it like a sparkler
on the 4th, as a flash of anger,
a snapshot of where we often go.

Albert's Hedge

Albert Hackers has drive,
he has goals to reach, promises to keep.
Albert doesn't stop.
He's always moving, shoving food
into his mouth, as if it were
his last meal, then belching
with a vengeance.

Albert doesn't say hello, he
enters the room with a lawn mower,
ready to cut, ready to edge.
He doesn't like questions, they
grow too fast and hit him in the face.
Don't ask him what he likes;
he doesn't know.

Albert keeps the hedges high
and trimmed good and thick. He
doesn't think anyone can
see through them. Albert
doesn't have time
for anything. If he can't do it
now, he can't do it. It has to be
done just so. He won't let the grass
grow, won't let the bushes
get out of shape.
He doesn't know he can.

Albert's Road

Albert doesn't like to see
where he's going. The wind-
shield wipers are too much
trouble, so he drives with big
drops of water clouding the way,
and pumps his brakes a lot. He
doesn't pay attention
at stop lights. One stop
isn't good enough. He'll stop
at least five times
'till he can't inch up any further.
The light turns green, and he
day dreams, doing his window shopping.

Two lanes aren't big enough
for Albert, he needs to drive
down the middle of the road
so he doesn't have to pay attention
to anyone else. Other cars don't
get in his way, he gets in theirs.
Albert drives an Oldsmobile, but
he thinks it's a Ferrari. He
thinks he's on a race track, and
he can take those curves, banked
or not, at fifty miles per hour.

Albert only uses his turn signal
when no one's around, he
wouldn't want to be polite.
It keeps the people who aren't watching
on their toes.

Break Up

We were down at the river that night. We could have been in his Chevy, or sitting at home eating *Haagen Dazs*. But *no*, he wanted to go down to the river. After dark. I never understand why he does anything. He never seems to have a reason. He just insists we go. I have to go along, willing or not. It's like he can't do it without me. There's some sort of glitch in his personality that requires him never to do anything alone. So I went. I followed him down to the river, and it was a beautiful night. The stars were out, it wasn't very cold. And the river was really racing because it had rained that day. And he stood there and he said, "This is it. I'm breaking it off. I've gotta be on my own." And I just laughed.

Feeling Raw

Like a woman
about to be bitten
by love,
I dig
my fingers
into deep pockets
of past pain
and wonderment.
My nails,
sharp and wild,
are clawing for warmth
and inclusion.
Snow has no mercy
on ears.
I hear
its silence covering
my world
like the coat
I wrap about me.
Better to feel
the cold
with my bare hands, than
nothing
at all.

In Black and White

I gaze at the child I used to be; she is cautiously smiling. The angels are looking for her. If she is the only one in the picture that is still alive, then where is she now? She seems like someone else.

In her twenties, a psychic will tell her she has a guardian angel, an American Indian who has been looking after her since she was five. Her brother, a smile in her childhood, will never make it past sixteen. There are other pictures: an aunt who will give her a bollo tie, and a grandfather she will never really know. This is where her father was born. This is where her grandfather will die.

She is on a family vacation in Colorado Springs, visiting relatives on her father's side. She is smiling only because the camera is aimed at her. I don't know what she is holding. Her forehead peeks from under straight, shiny hair, and she grasps something tightly as she leans against a wall. She seems unaware of the Indian seated beside her, her brother seated behind. I gaze at the child I used to be. If she is still alive, I need her now.

My Brother's Funeral

I walk down the stairs of my childhood home into a room full of small talk. People talk to fill the air. "It sure was a beautiful day yesterday."
"Yes, it was so warm."
They don't want to notice the emptiness, the words that hang on and pass. I can't ignore these things. I'm not good at small talk. I look for some distraction in meaning . . . why did it happen? Why?
But small talk is easier than answers. I forget how this silence will pass. I figure it's here forever.
The trick is to let go, let the silence be, let it tumble all by itself, down, down, down and come to a small halt on its own.

Warming Up to Death

I drive down Woodward at dusk
with Van Morrison's *Brown Eyed Girl*
transporting me back to sixteen
when I drove up and down Woodward
looking for boys. My eyes
are green, but I knew the song
was about me. I believed today
was the only day. The future
could be gone in a second,
like my brother was, in his
burgundy Skylark. I traveled
each day enclosed in a fog
of certainty that time
was inconsequential. Certain
if I really lived,
life would be taken away.

What is it like? To suddenly
not be able to drive down Woodward at dusk,
to not be able to hear *Brown Eyed Girl*.
Where does the music go?
My soul cannot exist
without the waves of song
that follow it even in silence.

At forty-three, I know
I have been here too long
to believe the music will leave me,
to believe I shouldn't live
just because it may be taken away.
Here, I float on asphalt, contented
with who I have become, securing
that song in my memory . . .
believing I will stay with this music . . .
longer . . . overcome thinkin' about it.

Stillness

I think I could always sit
in this nondescript morning,

patches of sun spewed on beige,
breezes filtered into birch.

Who knows what conquests
the real world has taken on,

what terror lies waiting
on streets not so far away.

I know there are lies and depression
growing in hearts that can't cope.

I know I am only this far
from their insanity bred by fear.

So I sit bravely, doing nothing
in hope of being one small wave

in a sea that needs this stillness.

Instructions from a Cat

Lounging in afternoon sun,
I keep the motor running
with eyes half open.
With a flick of the tail,
I can teach you to know
what you already know.

Never uttering a word,
I can undo a stranger.
It's the complex gone simple
that trips them up.

I go at it sideways
and rarely rub the wrong way.
Leaving the logic out
is the main idea,
padded feet are essential.

Now just ignore
what you thought you knew.

Unrestricted Acts

I am a maverick mustang with unshod hooves
that pound parched canyons drenched with sunlight.
I shake my mane at the breeze amidst
hundreds of transient seasons running wild.

I am a dwindling sunset arched in gold,
radiant with red, dressed in the silk of time,
ever moving with the wind, dropping behind horizons
like a cat's yawn, to sleep for awhile, then wake for more.

I am a passive pond mirroring stretches
of landscape drawn against the sky,
murky, moody with night, sparkling, hurried
with day, rippled by wind and swimming thoughts
learning to do the freestyle.

I am wild, slow, and hazy,
parched, radiant, and peaked,
as I move beyond control.

The Search

There's a bald spot on his head and she says she doesn't care. She's in her forties now and there aren't many men left. She thinks the guys worth knowing are already taken. So maybe it doesn't matter . . . about the bald spot.

She met him soon after her forty-second birthday. She had started dancing again, feeling like life was too short. Lucy joined her at the Silver Spur, and they started line-dance lessons. Every Friday night they learned a new dance, *The Matador, The Electric Slide, The Achy Breaky.* They stomped and kicked and shuffled their way to laughter on the dark, smoky, hardly-big-enough dance floor. When the lessons were over, they got to practice the newly-learned line dance a few times, but then sat watching the couples circle the floor doing the two-step with the band.

You had to have a partner to learn the two-step. She hadn't planned on this. She couldn't just ask someone to dance. She had to know how to do it first. And the guys all seemed to know who knew how to dance and who didn't. So Lucy inquired about the two-step lessons on Thursday nights. Did they have to have a partner? The verdict was, "not necessarily; just come. Marcy, the instructor, will find a partner for you." So they tried it.

Richard had a beard and a mustache hiding his face. He stood nervously with his hands in his pockets as the class began. He already knew the two-step but agreed to be her partner, when Marcy asked, and led her through the steps. He held her very lightly at arm's length and told her she was a natural. After the lesson was over, he danced with her some more.

"Where are you sitting? If you don't mind, I'll come and get you for a cha cha."

"Sure," she said. Though she wasn't so sure he would.

But he did. He came back again and again.

Even the following week and the week after that. He started out thanking her after each dance and walking away, but soon he hung around for a second or third dance. After awhile, he didn't walk away at all. He kept teaching her new steps.

"What do you do? Do you live around here?" She answered with one word sentences while trying to concentrate on the steps she was learning.

"You're really a good dancer for a beginner." He seemed so sincere.

More weeks passed, and he showed up even when she thought he would be working. He'd break away from his night job, as an engineer at GM, and spend his dinner hour with her. Then he'd leave again. In between weekends, she tried to imagine him without his beard. She tried to imagine him not dancing. She tried to imagine him in bed. If only he would stop talking, stop dancing, long enough for her to think about what else they could do together.

"What do you write about? Where have you danced before? Will you be here Good Friday?" he asked a lot of questions.

"Yes, yes, of course."

"We can't all be professionals," he said. "But you're a fast learner. If I didn't know better, I'd think you already knew how to do all these steps."

She smiled a lot at his compliments and grinned when he twirled her around. He'd look her straight in the eye, but always at arm's length. He never pulled her in closer.

"I'll walk you to your car." And then he walked away.

One evening they sat at a table catching their breath between dances, and she asked, "Have you ever been married?" He said he was in the process of a divorce. He didn't want to lose his three kids. He wanted them to go to private school, not be home schooled with his wife, who was very religious.

She thought this over and the next night asked, "Are you still living with your wife?"

"Yes," he said.

She thought maybe she didn't care. Maybe he would divorce. She had no desire to get married. She was getting old and liked to brush her teeth in private, go to bed at 10:30 if she felt like it. She wanted to have time to write, not schedule her time around someone else. She liked sleeping alone.

He talked about his kids a lot. They were still so young. He wanted them to have a father and know that he loved them.

And he wanted to know about her. Did she regret not having children? Did she care if he had a beer? Would she like to get something to eat? But he never came too close.

She was tired of the fragile egos of single men, the goodnight kisses that were only pleas for sex, the self-indulgent lack of dialogue. She thought back on Ken (who noticed she hadn't powdered her chin), and Tom (who drank too much), Ned (who only joked about marrying her).

Then they went for a bite to eat after dancing. She gave him her phone number. Instead of a hug one night, she kissed him. She wondered how any wife could do without a kiss like that. It was soft and warm. Or was it only for her? But she backed away and didn't ask a lot of questions. She kept dancing with him and let him grasp her hand. Then he went home to his own bed. She to hers. Maybe she had a bald spot too, in her heart, and she wasn't willing to grow anything there. She secretly wondered, would he leave his wife? Maybe he just wanted to dance. Maybe that's all he needed, with a bald spot on his head.

Over the Top

Mary Ann Wehler

Editors write on my work, *Strong words*. When I first started writing, I was uncomfortable and wondered: *Yes, but is it any good?* In a workshop, Naomi Shihab Nye, wrote: *You take on tough subjects*. I was proud. I search in my reading for affirmation to go on. Muriel Rukeyser said: *If one woman spoke the truth about her life, the world would split open*. Join me. Let's split false worlds.

My writing has started in the grandmother years of my life. Much of it comes from the power of memory and how that landscape worked in my life. If my writing helps a woman who is struggling, if it makes a difference, then I have found my audience. I hope as a writer that my truth is strong enough to be heard and to be useful.

The Scent of Mother

I remember the pungent smell of Mother. She was wearing her Playtex girdle, a wide elastic band, from waist to thigh. It held up her stockings with garters I could feel through her slip and house dress as I sat on the kitchen floor while she braided my hair. Her everyday worn-out girdle, it smelled of old rubber bands. But once, as I put my hands on her thighs to pull myself up, I got the scent of my mother down there. Again, I was playing a game on the floor; she was shelling peas at the white galvanized kitchen table. I walked my doll right up her leg. I smelled her personal smell. Somehow I knew that wasn't my odor to know, but I liked that smell. It was familiar, closely mine. Mother wore her girdle even in the hot summer; the smell of talcum powder filled the bathroom. It was necessary to dry hot sweaty skin to pull that rubber constraint up. I was curious about those wide-legged panties. I finally figured they made room for the garters. When I was invited to my first dance, my mother took me to Kresge's. I blushed as we stood in the aisle and she tried a garter belt over my clothes. She picked out my first nylons and held them next to my leg. I wished I were invisible. Later as I tried the contraption on in the privacy of my bedroom, I felt mysterious. And again at bath time, that private body smell, as I plopped in the prescribed two inches of water, and she warned me not to make waves that went over the top.

Obsessed by Ownership

My father bought ten acres on Hayes Road,
along the West Branch of the Clinton River.
Hauling a used garage from Detroit,
with a borrowed trailer and a prewar Model T Ford,
he mixed his own concrete for corner bolts and
raised the shelter, a castle for his kingdom.
Salvation Army metal cots made lumpy thrones
in cold or rain. My brother and I waved to our public
from the rumble seat, a worn blanket our mantle.
Each weekend, the old Ford stopped
at the broken cookie store on Groesbeck,
a dollar for a feast before the work began.
Mother made coffee with water from town.
My brothers and I had Kool-Aid and cookies,
sat at an old poker table on rickety folding chairs,
knights at the round table.
My parents, now serfs, started by cutting
three acres of grass. They hauled gravel
from the creek, filled in the washed out road.
They dug gardens: potatoes, corn, onions,
tomatoes, beans, radishes, peppers, peas, cabbage,
and three kinds of lettuce.
Every kind of tree that could make it in Michigan
was dropped in the ground, elm, oak, birch,
red maple, blue spruce, yellow chain,
pear, peach, plum, and apple.
They planted flower gardens,
filled with tulips, daffodils, petunias,
snap dragons, portulaca, and black-eyed Susans.
They dug a well that was often dry.
Five gallon buckets hauled water
from the well or creek to the gardens and trees.
They slaved on that property from April to November,
every Saturday and Sunday.

During the week, my father worked for General Motors.
We lived in an eastside rented flat.
Each spring, my mother scratched up the front yard dirt,
sprinkled seed, watered and weeded.
She washed side walks, swept porches,
shoveled the coal, dirt, and snow,
canned, ironed, sewed, cooked, washed dishes,
lit the tank, changed light bulbs, replaced faucet washers,
laid new linoleum, planted flowers, took out the papers,
scrubbed the floors, and walked long blocks
to shop for groceries. She painted over wallpaper
stretching a gallon over four walls.
My finger traced paper flowers through green paint.
Father came home, read the paper, ate dinner,
and slept in front of the radio.
The next weekend, they packed up, went back to the land,
where he sat in his Fifedom at the Round Table,
drinking hot coffee. He raised his cup, smiled and said,
I wonder what the poor people are doing.

Big Deal

I have a whispery recollection
of opening my bedroom door.
My father would be walking
through the hall to the bathroom.
Just a second's pause, in his undershirt,
no boxers covering his private parts,
Edna, do something, he would holler.
He looked mad at me, as if I'd
done something wrong.
My mom would come
and shoo me back in my room.
I laid in bed, needing to pee,
trying to figure out what I'd done wrong,
what was the big deal.

Pact

Skipping out at lunch time
in the eighth grade,
I took my pail
to Margaret Bombard's house.
We sat in the breakfast nook.
I ate my peanut butter
and jelly sandwich.
We hung upside down
on the benches,
while we were laughing
at how our faces looked,
she said,
I know how babies are made.
She told me
how my parents fertilized
the egg.
I thought that was
pretty disgusting.
Margaret and I made a pact
never to do *that.*
I broke my promise.

What Does it Take to be a Woman?

I liked to look through my mother's dresser. I was interested in the brassieres, slips with skinny straps, silky panties. She kept her nylons carefully between tissue in thin Hudson's boxes. Sachets in her drawers gave everything the light smell of violets. Her hankies were tied in a pink satin envelope with satin ribbon rosebuds on top. A tiny key was pinned inside with the handkerchiefs.

On rainy days, I would sit on my mother's bed and straighten out her jewelry box. I put the cuff links from her uniform next to the registered nurse pin. I matched up the jet beads with the onyx ring. I admired the filigreed silver setting with the blue sapphire hanging from a delicate chain. I tried on the tear drop crystal necklace without a clasp. The crystals looped over each other. I held the tear drop earrings in my hand, wondered about my mother's life, life before me, when she wore jewelry. I straightened out the gypsy necklace that I loved so much. Did she wear it dancing? Did she have other boyfriends? I pulled my dress-up clothes from the closet, put on her black chiffon dress with the twirling skirt and beaded bodice. I looked in the mirror and wondered who my lovers would be, who would dance with me.

When I was about thirteen, I realized the key with the hankies would open the sandalwood box on top of her dresser. One day, when I was home alone, I opened the box. Underneath birth certificates, baptism certificates, appliance sales slips, locks of hair and baby teeth, I found my mother's wedding certificate. It said my father had been married before. I was stunned. When she came home from the store, I asked her about it. She promised my father would explain when I was old enough. Ashamed, he never did.

My mother was ninety last year. We were going through her drawers, looking at some of the same jewelry I had fussed with fifty years ago. My father was dead. I asked what she knew about his first marriage. *He married a show girl. I looked like a show girl, but I was a nurse. He knew I'd stick around.*

No Down Payment

1959, I was sitting on the floor in the living room. The phone rang one hour after hookup. No living room furniture, that's why I sat on the floor. I was crying. The kitchen furniture didn't fit the way it seemed in the model. There wasn't room for two highchairs and a playpen. Looking out the window, I could see blocks of raped land, not a tree, not a bush, only curbs, and straw-filled clay holes for basements. 1959, no money down, G.I. loan, $100 a month for a three bedroom, 950 square foot house. I was sitting on the floor. At the third baby's baptism, I asked the priest's permission to use birth control. The priest said he would pray that I not get pregnant for a year. The baby was fussy. I jiggled him to settle down. I gazed through the doorwall of my corner lot. Two houses down the street were almost finished. I had no car. I was alone in my world. I plopped the baby in the playpen and ran for the bathroom. I sat on the ceramic tile that cost $200 extra, held onto the new white bowl and threw up. The baby screamed, the kids woke up, the two-year-old rattled her crib and whined. The boy walked out rubbing his eyes, hugged me and asked why I was crying in our new house. I was twenty-six years old. I had three kids and a house payment my folks thought was impossible. I made peanut butter sandwiches, put the babies in highchairs, the three-year-old on a telephone book. I was wiping the counter. I knocked the antique pitcher, a gift from my mother-in-law, onto the floor. While I swept up the china, I heard her voice say, *Smart Catholic girls do something to keep from getting pregnant*. I wiped messy mouths, changed diapers. Their father walked in. *What are you crying for? You're sitting in a nice new house*. I sobbed. *It's too small. The doctor called; the test was positive*. He threw his topcoat on the floor, shouted *JESUS CHRIST!*, and went back out the door.

In the Socket

She sent her babies down in the basement to play.
Shut the door and be quiet, she said. Her head whirled,
wondering how she could save life with their father.

He lay in bed in his overcoat, four in the afternoon,
hibernating from a job interview. She thought
she'd give him electroshock. Stick his toe in the socket.
You have to leave, she said.

Nothing wrong with me, his head under the pillow.
You're crazy! You'll never make it! he hollered as he
stumbled out of bed.

*If I make him leave, if I love him enough, if I'm lucky,
he'll stand up straight and come back to us*, she thought.
Get Out! she shouted. He left.

She wanted to climb in bed. Five babies waited
downstairs. She did what she had to do.
She changed the locks on the door, replaced
the shorted lightswitch, installed a new toilet.

Yet,
in the middle of the night,
she was still ashamed.
She had to give him up.

On Easter, My 90-Year-Old Mother Wondered, *Why Didn't You Go to Church?*

Bless me father. . .
The priest said, *You can't use birth control.*
The baby was born nine months later.
I cooked fish on Friday. My husband threw it away.
He wouldn't watch the babies. I dressed all five,
took them to church. He called me *Pope Mary Ann.*
He threw my scissors at me.
I was sewing clothes for the children and not screwing him.
I got a job. He lay in bed all day with his overcoat on.
I wanted to leave.
The church said, A *good Catholic wife stays.*
My father said, *You made your bed. Lie in it.*
My mother said, *God never gives more than you can take.*
My mother-in-law said (when the pie fell on the floor),
Did you do that on purpose?
My father-in-law hid his booze in my basement.
He was my only friend.
I talked to the doctor who prescribed Valium.
I went to the marriage counselor, who wanted two to come.
I went to the psychologist, who said it wasn't my problem.
I asked him to leave. He never worked again.
He lived at the Y, drank, smoked pot, took LSD.
He went away, never called, never wrote,
never sent his kids a card.
My father said, *I could have told you so.*

Father's Last Night

I lift the infant spoon to your mouth;
your throat works to swallow
like a worn faucet's drip
gurgling down a desert crack,
not getting to the root.
Clouds cover your eyes,
your lids flicker
with the effort to see.
You lie naked beneath the thinnest
soft white sheet,
while we attend you.
Mother dabs oil on your
shriveled penis. I recall
anointing my infants
with the same loving care she extends
this last night of your life.

Ninety-Year-Old Mother

She struggles over to the pool.
Both hands grip the walker.
She carries all her weight
along in her arms. Carefully,
she releases one hand, reaches
for the shining metal railing
that gleams down concrete steps.
She lifts one foot over the raised edge.
I watch her plant it firmly on the first
step. She stares at the ocean as if
thinking about gathering strength,
how she will lift her body and other
leg above that first rise. I hold her
hips and waist so she can feel secure.
After a bit, she grips the pool edge,
travels down the steps.
As water lightens her body, she sheds
the infirmity of ninety years like a second
skin. Her body enveloped in water,
she breathes a deep sign, looks at the sky
and palm trees. She says, *This feels*
wonderful! She holds my hands,
walking the width of the pool,
buoyed by water. Body light,
free from walker, cane, wheelchair,
she is released.

Dream Catcher

I immerse the grape vines in steaming water,
gently pushing them down into the wet,
encouraging them to bend and take the shape
of the tub. Their tentacles grasp and catch
at each other and my finger tips.

We dip our children into life.
Often, they resist the forms we have chosen.

Pulling and stretching their vines, I cajole
them around the frame. I struggle to
fit them on the circle. Concord, Thompson,
and Tokay; one would think it was in their
genes to be shaped, formed, and trimmed.
They have been trained in the vineyard for years.
Why do they resist?

We do the same with our young, hoping they
will take shape to our ways.

While the circle of vine dries, I choose beads to
thread on the yarn; golds, browns, ambers, and brass.
I prepare the yarn on a card, ready to weave.

It is easier to work with the vine than mold a child.

Each yarn woven circle has its own persona,
a bump here, a curlicue there.
Having worked the whole, I have no notion of
how or why it finished up the way it did,
as if the catcher had its own soul or spirit to choose.

Some Daughters Seem

untouchable.
I rock them
in the cradle
of my mind,
embrace them
in the chambers
of my heart,
hold their goodness
in my soul,
hear the hollow call
down
in their well,
ache
to lift them
over walls,
feel their pain
gnawing
in my gut,
look beyond
present sorrow,
will them
to stand
strong and healed.

My Son, David

I dream graffiti fills my house.
I open the door, walk onto the stage.
Tissue paper walls are wet with tears,
torn around the edges.
A steamer trunk, skull and cross bones on each side,
sits center stage. The front face is labeled:
Send to Bedlam, Care of David.
I wander around reading walls
covered with complaints.
I study etchings scrawled with black marker.
Fuck you. Die. Yesterday's Rock Star.
I come on David, sitting stage right.
I press his curly brown head to my chest.
Tears run down my face.

Awake, I'm stuck in a labyrinth,
searching for answers.
Scars of memories are etched in my soul.
I see the sunken eyes,
the maniacal look, the inappropriate smile.
Raw jagged words pitch out of his brain.
They travel through the air like spikes.

For My Daughter's Lost Baby

Flannery, Flannery,
where have you gone?
Are you dancing with angels?
Are you sleeping alone?
Flannery, Flannery,
Won't you come back?
Your Mother's been longing for you.

Flannery, Flannery,
where have you gone?
You're dancing with angels,
not sleeping alone.
Flannery, Flannery,
you're the breeze on her face,
and also the sun in her hair.

Coming Too Close

When I drove home that day,
the sun warmed my back.
I sang along with k. d. lang on tape.
Parking in the garage, I hollered a greeting to Jim.
Roaming in his own world, a day of rejection,
lost sales, he mistook my ardent greeting.
Thinking I'd yelled at him, he
spat the venom from his day in my face.
My heart was stunned, leaped in fits.
A chest full of pain devoured my joy.
Tears coursed down my cheeks.
As gravel under galloping horses
smashed about, so flew my heart.
Like the sand dollar washed up
by the sea, its center plucked
out by gulls, I was barren.
Next morning, I dressed, ate, drove to work,
aware that even my hands were numb.

Birth Coach To My Daughter

I wiped her sweating brow,
fought to hold her legs arched,
as his head began to crown.
She encouraged him on
with ancient straining calls.
I caressed his waxen body,
awed by my grandson's new strength.

I have no memory of my own deliveries.
I was drugged with Sodium Pentothal.
The doctor was in charge.
After carrying those children nine months,
I wasn't invited to their births.
Now, I know the wonder of delivering.

Tight Squeeze

I don't know why I can't choose the right size radiator cover for the kitchen floor vent. There has to be a cover; my grandson will fall in the vent. My husband will trip and break his leg. Maybe I bought the first one because it was attractive, shiny new and thin, not like the expanded me. Maybe it is because my mind keeps traveling back to my friends that are dying of cancer, going back to work, or worry/wondering about my adult children. I take the cover back. I bring the old cover with me this time. I exchange it for two pair of pea green socks at forty-one cents for the grandchildren, three shirts on sale (size ten). I don't know anyone size ten, and a new radiator cover, a plain one, not brass with shinny openings that baby fingers would poke into, not so shiny that it calls a curious child. I leave my old cover in the checkout lady's waste basket. I bring the new cover home. It is two inches too long, like the note I got from a friend who is stuck in a thirty year old glue pot. I can't pull her out. I can't change the way she sees. It won't fit. I try to push it into the opening, unbelieving. I lift it up, look at the hole, look at the cover, how can this be? I try one more time, it is at least two inches too long. My husband asks, *Will you be back on Saturday in time for dinner?* I feel the leash. He wants to connect. *Eat with the guys, I might stay in Ann Arbor,* I say. I resist yelling, *Give me some space.* I seem to want more and more. As the children leave the house I spread farther, like rolling hot lava. I box and bag the radiator cover to take back again. I chant my mantra 4" x 10", 4" x 10". I will try once more. Monday I go back to work. I will be forced into a time schedule 4 x 10, a curriculum 4 x 10, a dress code 4 x 10. No matter if I'm 3 x 14 or maybe 4 x 12, just a little bit different. I have to squeeze into the space allotted. Run on someone else's time, or fit into someone else's shirt.

Marcia's Chair

She was fire, she was water,
she was dance, she was dream.
We danced on Torch Lake's sands
in batiste, antique gowns.
She challenged me, taught me
the joy of being a person,
more than mother, daughter, teacher.
She pulled me to the theater,
when snow had closed the schools.
We never ate at the same restaurant,
shopped at the same store.
We talked and talked, listened and listened.
We digested each other's thoughts.

Her wallet carried the best plastic
surgeon's number, when we were thirty-eight and forty.
I promised to go with her before we turned fifty.
Once, she went to the surgeon alone.
It was her nose. It tilted to the right.
I could not see it. I guess the doctor
couldn't either. He sent her home.
But she didn't want to get old.
She hung herself with two of her husband's ties.
Just hooked them around the bathroom door
and her neck, kicked the chair out.
She was forty eight.

I always thought we'd still be talking over coffee at eighty.
Now I'm sixty; she's gone. I still see her in the back
of her sailboat at the tiller, walking down the path
at my wedding, a little swagger in her stance.
I still feel her in the tearoom at the art museum.
Everytime I go to the theater, I think of her.
Why did she have to be so dramatic?

Not Fair

I step into hell,
my dear friend's house. She is swirling
up in the smoke of chemotherapy.
The blossom of her smile has faded.
Her sweet bald head gleams in the afternoon sun.
A few blond hairs peek out from her scalp,
hairs finer than a gossamer spider web.
Her pink ears are thin and translucent
like grandma's best bone china cup.
Her shorts and shirt are loose leaves around a brittle stalk.
She holds her honeycombed spine carefully erect,
a mismove could crumble her fragile back.
I must eat my watermelon, she says quietly in the kitchen.
The morphine isn't working, the pain is relentless.
I focus on her hollow pale blue eyes and listen.
I'm angry, really angry! she murmurs.
I struggle with words to comfort her suffering.
It's not fair; I'm afraid to sleep, she whispers,
I dreamed a machine came down from the sky
and cut my breast off.
There is a hungry look on her face,
pleading for more time.
Her eyes ask me for something I cannot give.
My heart grips, my stomach churns,
and my soul cries silently, *Let go*.

Make These Signs Yours

Aline Soules

My ideas come from looking through an internal telescope where a small fact or image unlocks my understanding of the larger world. I am fascinated by small works of art—Holbein miniatures, Rajput paintings, Haiku, a child's focus on ordering a tiny piece of the universe while everything around is chaotic. The stories behind these works also attract me. Holbein, for example, was sent to paint Anne of Cleves so Henry VIII could decide whether or not to marry her. The miniature Holbein painted was so colored by his falling in love with his subject that Henry brought Anne to England and history was changed. A piece of the larger world catches my attention and I turn it around to mirror the larger world back again. These connections are what I try to enfold and unfold in my work so that a sense of order emerges and the significance of patterns is revealed.

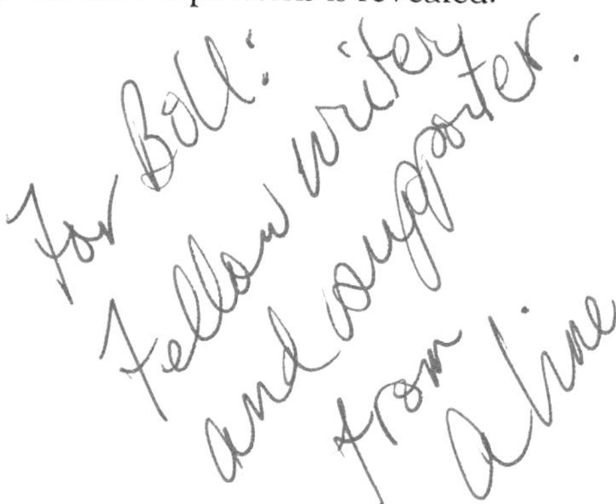

Back Porch

A back porch is honest.
Old rambling roses
you planted when you moved in
crawl untended up its poles
and trail over the roof.
The wooden planks are cracked
and the flaking paint is splotched
with green and red
from your children's paintbox.

Slouched on an old chair
no longer good enough
for the living room,
you don't worry about
offending sensibilities
with old work clothes or dirty boots.
You relax with a cup of tea,
leave a wet ring on the sloping floor
and smell the roses with the chicken
roasting for dinner in the kitchen beyond.

Leaning back, you think
about nothing and everything—
when your son is due back
from hockey, the light
through the rose petals, the diet
you'll never start, the last time
you made love.

As the sun slants deeper,
shadows lengthen across the floor
and mingle against the sides
of the house—roses, the chair,
the poles that connect
the railings to the roof,
and you.

Let's Just Go On

When we emigrated to Ontario
from Scotland, I was a teenager.
We miss the hills and the sea, said Mother,

laying the groundwork for our first
and future summer vacations.
Mother and I went while Father worked.

She drove and I read the maps.
We camped to save money, but ate in restaurants
as she had to do all the driving.

The first summer, she told my father
we were going to the Smoky Mountains
in Tennessee. We slept by a bear trap.

A day or so later, she looked at the maps.
It's not that far to the sea, she said,
Let's just go on. We sent postcards from Florida.

The next year, she told my father
we were going to the Black Hills
in South Dakota. We lost our tarp to hailstones.

A day or so later, she looked at the maps.
It's not that far to the sea, she said,
Let's just go on. We sent postcards from San Francisco.

We saw forty-eight states and ten provinces
in five years. I got to be the best map reader around,
and Father stopped asking where we were going.

Washday

She bends her head
over the gray tub
and rubs a flannel shirt
against the washboard.
The rat-a-tat of her knuckles
beats out dirt
with water and thick suds,
stripping lint and color
from the tired cotton plaid.

All the while, a man
rains words on her head
like the water
that pulses unchecked
down the washboard.
His harsh percussion rises
and falls with a rhythm
that matches her pumping arms
and shaking body.

She lifts the stopper
in the sink. Water swirls
down the drain, sucks away
dirt and used-up suds, but
leaves angry words
like a soap film
on the faded plaid
that will no longer
rinse clear.

Paper Cups

I don't know why I took them home
after Mother died. They were hidden
in a kitchen cupboard and it seemed a shame
to waste them. She would have approved.
I put them away and forgot them.

Today, it is my turn to serve
the boys at soccer. I cut up oranges,
grab water jugs and find
the cups.

I sit through the game with its noise
and dirt and knobby knees, but
I think about the cups as I wait for half-time.
A butterfly weaves in
and out of the boys' legs.

The whistle blows. The boys
engulf orange quarters with their fists,
squeezing sweet juice into their mouths.
They gulp cool water from the cups
and pour it from the cups onto their heads.

The game ends. The butterfly is gone.
I pick up sticky rinds and scrumpled cups
tossed by boys Mother never met,
in a place she never saw, in a time
she never knew.

Links

With your infant mouth
round my nipple, we are one,
as I was one with your father
the moment you began.

I feel your tug
as we rock under the old quilt.
Unclear shapes
loom in the dim light—
crib, dresser, shelves,
a mis-shapen box.

Downstairs, snores mingle
with the hum of the fridge,
the guinea pig
rustles his cedar-shaving bed,
and air rushes from the grate
as the furnace kicks in.
The smell of fried onions
lingers from supper.

Outside, leaves respond
to the growing wind,
while trucks whine
on their journey up the freeway,
and trains crash
in the freightyard a mile away.

Thunder closes in.
Lightning casts eerie shadows.
Fat rain spats the sidewalk
and the smell of just-damp earth
seeps through the open crack
in the bedroom window.

The half-light of street lamps
diffuses under clouds
that hide distant stars and planets,
but the moon finds a narrow path
through the storm to find
your face.

Nothing changes your rhythm,
eyes and fists clenched,
brow sweating with effort,
center of the universe.

Clocks

I remember clocks from my childhood.
They were supple and willing to compromise.
They let me find long trails in the woods,
tiny crabs in seapools, dreams in books
on a summer day. Now they are forever
draped on easy chairs, wrapped around swings,
flexed over tree limbs.

I have left them behind and gone on,
on to new clocks, clocks that have
taken over. They make me get up,
eat breakfast while I pack lunch,
set out meat to defrost for dinner,
speed to work, hurry to meetings,
rush to pick up my child, fix dinner
in twenty minutes, go to bed by ten
so I can lie awake, waiting for them
to claim me in the morning.

One day, I'll show them. I'll tear them
from the walls and toss them in the trash.
I'll walk to the shore to find
a sailboat creaking in the bay.
If any of them rise and follow me,
it won't matter. I'll cast off and set my course
for the rose and gold, leaving them
bobbing in my wake as I grow smaller
and smaller in the deepening night.

Great Minds Think Unlike

Ethel and Ruth sit in Ruth's kitchen
drinking coffee and contemplating.

The refrigerator door has fallen off.

The hinges, loose for some time,
have finally given way.

They have propped the door back
with a large boulder from the garden.

Now, they sip in silence, facing each other,
elbows propped on the table.

Ethel thinks about how long the food
will stay cold, who can fix the fridge,
what word she should look up
in the yellow pages.

Ruth wonders how to decorate the rock.

A Dozen Shirts

We used to get together
over shirts, remember?

You came and cleaned,
while I ironed the shirts
our husbands wore to play
and war and work.

In the heat of the summer,
we waited, and talked
over the roar of the vacuum
and the clump of the iron
on a sleeve.

*

Pilgrims take
six months to make
a woolen shirt—
to shear the sheep,
to card and spin,
to weave the cloth,
to cut and stitch,
to give the shirt
to someone they love.

*

Mr. Reale gives away
white t-shirts stamped in red
with REALE CEMENT (the R
in a crown) and 282-2369.

They match his truck.

The boys on his soccer team
will be good advertising
until the Clorox white turns gray
and the red letters flake with age
to read
RE   CE NT or
  ALE MENT or
RA   T.

*

She takes the shirts
from his side of the closet,
the pin stripes, the solids,
the button-down oxfords,

and folds them neatly
in brown paper bags
to wait for the pick-up
on Tuesday.

She spreads her own shirts
across the length of the rod.
With all that space, they
will never be crushed again.

*

As a Boy Scout grows,
his shirt grows with him.

Its plain brown cloth
stretches and bends

as he climbs and camps
and lifts newspapers

to earn a merit badge
for the sleeve.

*

If a knock on the door
comes at midnight,
people don't answer.

It might be the brown shirts
to drag them from bed
and put them in trucks
for the ovens.

*

It is the morning of Tuesday,
January 30, 1649.
King Charles I wears two shirts
against the chill. *The people must not*
think I am afraid, he says,
as they lead him to the scaffold
to bloody both the shirts
with an axe.

*

See the shirts.
They are white.

See the men,
Blue and Gray.

See them fight.
See them fall.

Hear the pain.
See the gall.

See the women
tear the shirts.

See the women
stem the blood.

See the shirts.
They are red.

See the men.
They are dead.

*

High flyin'
struttin' the street
flashin' a smile
cravin' the looks,
the praise,
the envy—
shot for a silk shirt.

*

When light dawns and the wind begins
to bluster, the scarecrow
puffs his chest and stretches billowed arms
over the corn's swaying leaves.

All day, he flaps, worn reds
and yellows driving the crows away.
All day, they struggle. The field
is endless motion. At last,

the light fades and the wind falters.
He shrugs a few more times, then
drops his flannel arms. Slumped
into his chest, he rests.

Tomorrow, he must rise early
to answer the unceasing call.

*

I don't want a new shirt
I want my old one,
the one that knows me
so well
it lies against
the curves of my skin
like a lover.

*

When my shirt has to go, I shall
cut two pieces from its back
to make a little elephant
for the baby across the street,

and I'll take its right front
to polish the table in the hall
while its partner mops
the oil off the garage floor.

I'll fold its sleeve in half
as a chin rest for my son's violin,
and the other can hang as a windsock
to waft out its song on the breeze.

Whole Woman

After surgery, Ruth said no
to all the devices the doctors
and nurses and social workers offered.
She went to the store
and bought man's shirts,
thick and flannel for winter.

When her hair began to fall out,
leaving stringy gray tufts,
she made an appointment
to get it cut off. Her hairdresser
couldn't bring herself to do it,
so she went to a barber,
an ex-marine who knew what to do.

When children stared, she smiled
and waved and said *it's okay*.
When clerks were unsure
how to serve her in stores,
or shied away, or dropped their eyes,
she held up her head and carried on
without missing a beat.

She found out which of her women
friends would go with her
to a concert or a play. When she died,
she left letters naming them
pallbearers.

Make These Signs Yours

Play music that's sunshine
on a red tile floor.

Watch light sparkle wine
in a glass.

Peel an apple
so its spiral drops whole
to the plate.

Mark Sunday in slow time.

When the peony blooms,
breathe its scent all day.

Make these signs yours.

Whether they come
in yellow woods or dark days,

seize them as your own. Some day,
they will fit together in ways
you never imagined,
make patterns you never saw,
and reveal a truth
you never knew.

Copier Man

With only five minutes until his meeting and no secretary in sight, Norman ran to the workroom to make a quick copy of his report. Glancing down at the still warm pages, he read:

Hi! My name is Pannox 500. What's your name? Put your answer on my glass plate and press the button.

"Who the hell is fooling with the copy machine," he thought.

He fed it in again. The first page looked fine, then he checked page 2.

You have a long name, it said, *or is it just 'Report on Robotronics, Inc.?'*

"This is ridiculous," he thought. He fed in page 2 again.

Didn't you just give me that page? Or do you work for Robotronics, Inc.?

Sweat popped out on his forehead and in his armpits. "Great," he thought, "just what I need." He tried page 3.

I don't understand. Your last page started in the middle of a sentence. And it didn't answer my question!

His collar tightened, but he gave it one more try. Success! His neck returned to normal size. On the way out the door, he turned and stared at the copier one more time.

All through the day, he couldn't get the Pannox off his mind. Later that afternoon, he strolled by the workroom and watched people going in and out to the copier. Drone, drone, drone. The pages soldiered on, one after the other.

"Hi, Norman, need something?" asked Cathy, his boss' secretary.

"No, I was just looking for a pen." Norman went over to the cabinet and got out a couple. "By the way, have you had any trouble with the Pannox today?"

"No. Why?"

"I had to copy a couple of sheets in a hurry this morning and I could only get every other one to work. I guess it had a hard time getting up this morning."

Cathy laughed. "I guess so. It's fine now."

Back at his desk, Norman took the strange pages from the drawer where he had hidden them and stared.

A call near the end of the day kept him late. When he was finally ready to leave, he had to pass by the workroom again. The lights and the

Pannox were both off, but he decided to turn them on. When the Pannox had warmed up, he ran a blank page through the feeder.

I read your last page this morning. That didn't tell me anything either! Are you playing games with me, Report?

He grabbed another blank piece of paper. "My name is NOT Report," he wrote, "it's Norman Brown and I want you to quit talking to me. Now!" He bunged it through the feeder.

I thought your name was Report! You lied to me! How dare you! You're lucky I let you copy anything this morning. If you don't treat me right, I won't let you copy anything again!

"That's just fine with me. I don't usually copy things anyway. It was just that I was in a hurry this morning. This is the last you'll see of me, believe me!"

Norman jammed the page through the feeder and grabbed the hot copy as it rolled from the machine. It was blank. The writing on the original was as bold as ever. He went to throw away the copy, then changed his mind and put it in his briefcase.

Two days later, he placed some papers he wanted copied in the typing pool box. About 2 p.m., Cathy stopped by.

"Excuse me, Norman, but I'm afraid I won't be able to copy your papers this afternoon. Something's gone wrong with the Pannox. I added more toner, but all I'm getting is a blank page. Will tomorrow be soon enough?"

Norman stared and felt his neck start to swell again.

"Norman?"

"Oh, sure, that'll be fine. I don't need them until Thursday."

Later that day, he found an excuse to stop by Cathy's desk.

"The Pannox fixed yet?" he asked.

"You know, it's funny you should ask. I was talking to Joan, you know, David Bell's secretary. She didn't know it wasn't working and she went in and it copied fine. I had the man in anyway, but he couldn't find anything wrong. I'll get your papers done first thing in the morning."

"Thanks. That'll be great." Norman felt slightly queasy, but passed by the workroom and refused to go in.

Next morning, Cathy was back at half past nine.

"I'm sorry, Norman, but the Pannox is acting up again. We can't figure it out. It works sometimes, but not others. I'll see if I can do your papers this afternoon."

"That's okay. Why don't you give them back to me and I'll go to PrintOver and do them on my lunch hour. I've decided they need to go out today after all."

"Okay. Just get a receipt and I'll give you the money out of petty cash."

There was a line at the print shop and it took Norman most of his lunch hour to get his copies. As the next two weeks went by, he found himself going there regularly or asking someone in the typing pool to go for him. Pretty soon, the word got around.

"Hey Norman, better disguise your stuff!" "Hey Norman, I guess the Pannox doesn't like you!"

He wouldn't have minded the teasing if it had just been a coincidence, but somehow, he knew it wasn't. One night, he stayed late to talk to the Pannox.

"Why are you doing this to me?"

Doing what?

"You know. I need copies of things and you won't do it. Why me? Why not somebody else? Why not everyone?"

I'm tired and lonely, Norman. I need a friend. People come in here all the time and copy, copy, copy. They talk to each other, but they never talk to me. They don't even know I exist. You all go off somewhere at night and leave me by myself. So one night, I decided to talk to the very first person that came in next morning. That was you, Norman.

"Okay, just this once, I'll talk to you."

Well, I don't know now. If you don't want to talk to me, we can always go on as we are.

"No, please, really. I mean, I've changed my mind. It's just that I'm busy, so I can only talk to you this one time. Okay?"

Okay, so tell me, what do you do when I'm not here?

"I'm a bit like you. I live by myself too. I like to read."

That's funny. I hate to read. Reading is so boring.

"Not to me it isn't. My mother used to say 'If you've got a book, you've got a friend.' You can read something and escape into another world."

Why do you want to do that? You're in the same world.

"Believe me, it's not all it's cracked up to be. Besides, I don't read reports and papers at home. I read stories."

What are stories?

"They're pretend. People make them up for fun or to explain their ideas about things or people."

I don't understand.

"I can't explain."

Show me one.

"I don't have one with me, but I'll make you a deal. If I bring you one tomorrow, you'll start making copies for me and you won't bug me after that. Okay?"

Okay.

That night, Norman tried to find a book Pannox would like. This was not easy, but he found a story about clones that he thought maybe a copier could relate to. He began to feed it into Pannox after work the next day. He stopped after Chapter 1.

"Well, what do you think?"

Very interesting. Is that the end?

"No, but I don't have time to feed you the whole story. Besides, my finger is killing me from pushing this damn button."

I like Arlene Clone. I wish I had a clone. Get me a clone, Norman.

"I can't get you a clone. This is fiction—pretend—made up. It isn't real."

Tell me the rest of the story.

"I haven't time now."

You want your copies?

"You promised."

I lied.

"We had a deal, remember?"

You lied to me once about your name so I get to lie to you once. I want the rest of the story.

"Okay, let's make another deal—for real this time. I'll feed you the rest of the story, a chapter every night until it's done, and after that you'll leave me alone. Oh, wait a minute—not Tuesdays. I have to go to my mother's—every night but Tuesdays. Is it a deal?"

Okay.

"You're not lying?"

No.

"Okay. Tomorrow."

Norman came every night but Tuesdays and fed Pannox the rest of the twenty-eight chapters. He started padding his finger with a bandage to stop it from getting any worse. They talked about each chapter for a little while before Norman went home. After the story was finished, Pannox asked for another one.

"I thought we had a deal."

I know, but I want another one.

"You're not going to go back on your deal, are you?"

No.

"Okay, we're done, right? You won't bug me any more, right?"

Did you know David Bell is getting a promotion?

"How do you know that?"

Come on, Norman. You're not stupid. I see all the papers in this place, don't I?

Norman stopped in the middle of pressing the button.

"Do you know why I didn't get mine?"

Do I get another story?

Norman thought for a while.

"Okay, one more story, but you tell me about my promotion and about David's. Then you leave me alone. Deal?"

Deal.

After the second book, Norman found out why he didn't get his promotion.

Get a new suit, Norman, and quit wearing bow ties.

After the third book, Norman found out that David Bell was seeing the boss' daughter. After the tenth book, he knew more about what was going on in the company than his boss.

Get me a clone, Norman.

"I told you ages ago, I can't get you a clone."

Sure you can, Norman. Look how much more copying has been going on in the last few weeks.

"That's because I keep copying books for you. It doesn't count."

Maybe not, but they know they're using more paper. Get me a clone, Norman.

"There's no way. Besides, I don't want them paying attention to all the extra copying I'm doing."

Want to know how to get your promotion?

Norman prepared a report arguing for an additional copier and submitted it to his boss. That evening, after Norman had fed in another chapter, Pannox said:

That report looked good. The only thing is you didn't tell them what kind to get. I want a nice one with form feeding, sorting, enlarging, reducing . . .

"You'll be lucky to get anything, you damn greedy machine."

But in a few weeks, a new copier was installed with all the latest features. That night, Pannox said:

You're a good guy, Norman. You can call me Pan. By the way, that's a great suit. The tie's not so bad either.

"Never mind that. What about my promotion?"

Why don't you get an account going with Sarten's?

"Never heard of it."

That's just the point. Not many have. But I saw a report that said they're going to be big.

"Thanks, Pan. You can call me Norm."

Over the next couple of years, Norm and Pan read and read and read. At first, Pan just liked sci fi stories with machines—I, Robot or 2001—but later, after putting some of the ideas together, he started to be interested in people too and then Norm could read him anything. In the meantime, Norm bought three suits, started several accounts, and was promoted twice. The workroom was expanded to incorporate two additional smaller copiers, including one that handled color.

I want to see your face, Norm. Show me your face.

Norm shut his eyes tightly, pressed his face into the glass and pushed the button.

That's funny, you look flat-faced, sort of squished.

Next day, Norm brought a photo instead.

You look better today, Norm, much better.

"Thanks."

But I don't feel so hot. I'm kind of tired. Maybe we should just skip our chapter tonight. Okay?

"Sure, whatever you want. I'll see you tomorrow."

Over the next few weeks, Pan skipped quite a few chapters and began to have trouble making it through the day. The repair man was called in a number of times, but eventually he just shook his head.

"This baby's had it," he said. "Gotta go."

Norm went back to his office. It had just been re-decorated with wood paneling and thick blue carpeting. He rocked back and forth in his swivel chair. How was he going to find out what was going on? What would he do? Who would he read with? Who would he talk to?

"How you feeling?"

Not good, Norman. Not good.

"They're going to take you away tomorrow, you know."

Yes, I know. They wrote a memo about it today.

"I'll miss you."

That's okay. It's been a good life and you've made it better. You got me a whole family. You've been a friend. Thanks, Norm.

"You're welcome. You've been a good friend too. No one's ever talked to me about books the way you have and you've helped me get ahead. Thanks, Pan."

You're welcome. Before we say goodbye, I've got one more thing to tell you. You should put on one of those fancy suits and ask Cathy out to dinner.

Norm smiled. Maybe he would.

Goodbye, Norm.

"Goodbye, Pan."

Norm turned Pan off for the last time, switched off the lights and went home.

The next day, they took Pan away and brought a replacement. Norm had a tough time for a few weeks. He missed a deadline on the company contract with Sarten, he didn't have the details he really needed during the big meeting with FlexTop. Maybe he's burned out, they said. Tired, you know. But Norm wasn't tired. He began to wonder what to do. One night, after staying late, he passed by the workroom. He turned on the lights and looked at the four machines sitting in the middle of the floor. For old times' sake, he turned one on, the little color one. He took a blank page, wrote on it and pushed it into the feeder.

Hi? My name is Norm. What's yours? Print your answer on the copy and roll it into your tray.

Eyes Open to the Deep Green Lake

Susan Knoppow

The wonder of poetry is that it takes me places I had no idea I needed to go. I may sit down to write about the tree outside my bedroom window, but by the time I reach the tenth draft, I've wandered away from the yard to explore my relationship with last Tuesday's lunch partner, and why the tomato soup was so hot, and what that does or does not have to do with my plans for the future.

I've grown to love revision, the opportunity to turn a word or emotion over and over in my hand like a stone until I find just the right way to express what I mean. It sometimes requires fictionalizing or intensifying my original words, but revision nearly always leads to greater clarity. I may not report what "really" happened, but I try to make sure that those who read my poems grasp the intention behind my lines.

I tell more of the truth and less of the truth than any of us expects. I like it that way.

Making Babies

The way I learn about babies
is this:
One afternoon in the car
Dad and me and Ellen
in the front seat
with no radio
waiting
with the door open,
he says it's seeds
and close
and love.
He says the love part
twice, but I remember seeds
best of anything.

The way I understand about babies
is this:
Another afternoon walking
home from first grade
alone, and a boy I know runs
across the yard
almost to the corner
where we cross.
He makes a circle
with two fingers
and wiggles another
finger in and out and in
and out and in and I
can't forget the sun
and the grass
and his blond hair
and feeling very small.

Easy as Breath

I was eighteen—too old
for a first kiss.
He taught swimming
and had the deep smooth
body of a young man
who could rescue
a drowning child.

So when he touched my hand
like a question that summer
I followed
from the camp kitchen
through the broken
screen door
past sleeping children
in their cabins
to the edge of the woods.

I still know
the flatness of it,
the electricity
behind my knees,
the tang of his breath
like tasting metal.

Street Signs

The red poncho lady haunts these streets too.
Winter or spring, I pass her most evenings
when all I want is a little exercise
before dinner. But the city blocks
talk back, their tangled gardens,
the mailboxes chained to trees looming
urban and so ordinary, I know one day
the poncho lady could follow me home,
dump her parcels on my kitchen floor
then leave. Some days she is yellow
or green, always a sight in smudged lipstick
and huge hoop earrings, clutching
plastic grocery bags stuffed with a rainbow
of clothing. But really, she doesn't shock me
as much as the two little girls who dance all summer
in their chain-link yard, their lips smeared
that same anxious shade. On them it's a pout,
a promise they'll grow into like their stuttering
dance, narrow hips and shoulders shimmering
in the dusky light of pre-teen desire.
Armed with sticks and bits of cheese, the girls break
from their routine to taunt a local stray
who tolerates their attention in the same detached
manner she once seduced me
into watching her eat a sparrow.
Paws firm on the tiny chest, the cat nibbled and licked
at the bird who lay there blinking, stunned
but not quite dead. It was the only time the poncho lady
spoke to me. *This is what we do*, she said,
her voice low as charred velvet. *It's all we know.*

Swimming the Lake

A girl I hate, who turns cartwheels
across the soccer field
on our way to general swim,
tells me I have perfect legs,
keyholes at knees, calves and thighs
when I stand straight. But boys
at this overnight camp
are learning to hold breasts,
new moons in their twelve-year-old hands.
She has them, and I don't. We both know
that empty space, no matter how perfect
is no good in wooded darkness. Night here
stretches long and deep as Elk Lake,
where mornings we meditate water,
swimming laps back and forth
beside the weathered dock
until the lifeguard's whistle
startles us from reverie
and we are reduced again
to children in flowered suits
shivering in the sun's flat face.
I want to swim across this summer,
to kick from here to the far beach.
My legs ache in anticipation of the last day
when a counselor in a rowboat
will follow with life vests as we pull ourselves
toward the other shore,
eyes open to the deep green lake
as though in our whole lives
there could be nothing more dangerous
than drowning, as though
we could swim like this
beyond adolescence and emerge
glittering, dripping wet on the other side.

Deep Black Pine and Paper Birch

Pictured Rocks National Lakeshore

This weekend drips with spider webs,
blueberries and lady fern, misty beaches
at midnight, soggy pancakes.

Superior is north
where we left it minor highways ago.
Standing in that great lake, on rocks
the size of blue fists
I could feel my skin breathe.

Now, southbound over Mackinac,
sand between my toes,
hair full of campfire and damp leaves
I look down through the bridge
and read Lake Michigan between the lines.
Dusty green, it rolls toward shore like a slow tongue.

These days are made of water.
Liquid shadow and reflection
rain into deep black pine and paper birch.
All the way home
I recollect waterfalls and rainstorms.

Star Bakery

A woman with a pale smile points to onion rolls. *Six of the darker ones,* she says. *Near the front.* She scowls and jabs at the glass case. *These here. And those.* The bakery lady is Russian. She is slow today, exhausted by the women who choose onion rolls like jewels. She fills a paper sack for two dollars, slides it across the counter, then turns to her next customer. *One challah,* the woman says, her voice like a bird's. *A fresh one.* She scans the rows of identical braided loaves. *That one there. I like to make a nice cheese sandwich for lunch, you know.* I'm next in line, and ask for a seven layer cake, pale yellow with chocolate icing, like my grandmother bought from this bakery every Friday afternoon. *How much?* asks the clerk, and I pause. I have never seen this cake anywhere but on my grandmother's table. A year after her death, I'm here alone. Does it come in inches? Should I ask for slices? Pounds? Should I want an end piece, or is the middle best? The bakery lady waits, eyeing the lengthening line of customers behind me. *This much,* I say at last, falsely confident, my hands wide apart. *Extra icing, too. But not that squashed piece on the end . . .* She looks up for barely a moment, pads the box with tissue, then ties it all with string. I am initiated into the world of Jewish baked goods for less than a dollar's worth of pastry.

It's Always a Quarter to Four in My Kitchen

The clock on the stove
stopped one afternoon in late fall
while a woman
stirred soup for dinner. She didn't notice
the yellow hands, still, stuck
on nine and four. It wasn't a meal that needed
a clock—she cooked and tasted
until her soup was warm, the salad dressed,
the butter soft. And then she ate,
alone, at a quarter to four.

I sit where she sat, in my clean, broad kitchen. I try
to change the time, to clean the grease
from the grooves of the small black knob. But this clock
will not be moved. I sit with my soup and wonder
about the woman before me who let the time stand still.

Paperweight

This heart is not an egg. This blue
heart, heavy as stone, fits in my palm,
more perfect than the finger with which I trace
Baccarat in tiny script along one edge.
I smudge this gift with fingerprints,
risk dropping it to the wooden floor.

But this heart,
blue as rain, blue as lost crayons
or spent blood, would not crack
like an egg, would not bleed. It holds light
like I hold your son, reflects objects
on my desk—a flower pot
filled with pens, a half-finished letter
to thank you for dinner the night
rain hurled itself against the windshield,
and it felt like riding through the car wash
when I was small, certain
that if water rushed in
I would be the only one swept away.

We reached home as the storm
settled like a sigh, and you smiled
to see me cradling the heart on my lap
as though I needed to protect anything so strong.

Ways to Go

The woman extracts a noose from her bag,
then a child-proof medicine bottle, a toy car,
a paring knife, a plastic gun. It's Saturday night,
the play *Ways to Go*, in which a woman,
alone on stage, surrounds herself
with deadly objects, then sits and stares
and doesn't die. From her audience,
at first laughter, but the woman
is stone. She examines the knife, touches the blade
to her wrist, then sets it back
among the invitations before her.
I am mesmerized by her disregard
for the audience, which shifts nervously
at the dangerous lack of spectacle. People leave
as they realize there will be no intermission, the lights
don't go back up. But I keep my place. I know
what happens next, whether or not it unfolds
on this stage. If you were here with me,
you would know too.

Scene two: our mother
alone in her darkening kitchen, absentmindedly
shreds tissues as she tries not to stare
at the princess phone stage right.
When the call comes, it is from an emergency room doctor
or a frightened roommate. Mother asks one question,
then hangs up. This scene repeats. Next, the sister
cleans out the woman's apartment. That would be me
finding your stuffed tiger under a pillow,
broken glass in the sink, three tall plastic cups
and a bottle of vodka empty enough
that you really could have died this time.

But our lives are not a play. We know too well
the fold of a hospital sheet, the blue plastic tip
of an IV tube. Our intimacy is in these details,
in the tender vein at the back of your hand,
in rare moments alone like last Sunday
on the library steps past midnight
where we shared a sno-cone, sticky as a sour kiss.
Lemon's better than the other flavors,
you told me. *You never know
what to expect*. Which is why
I need more nights like that one,
its sweet lemon melting between our fingers
as I memorized the small bones of your hand,
the ragged cuticles and the way a gold band
slips about your finger, secure but never certain.

I can tell you *Ways to Go* closes
as the woman pulls a blanket over her head. She rocks
slowly until the theater is nearly empty.
You can leave anytime, she says,
so I stay.

Snapshots: Women with Strawberries

A woman kneels
among rows of fruit.
It is June, but she
is pregnant and chilly,
her fingers numb. Carefully
she chooses strawberries
like kisses
for her new baby.

A woman picks
through green plastic baskets,
berries under stiff cellophane
secured with rubber bands.
She is looking
for treats
for her grandchildren
who may not visit
on Sunday.

A woman sits alone
at a long wooden table
with a bowl
of strawberries
sliced open
pale and vulnerable
as the inside of a lip.
She eats them
with a spoon.

Barbie Clothes

Kathy, the biggest baby-sitter, brings me a long blue box of Barbie clothes she made for sewing class. My favorite is the Barbie bath mat from a strip of someone's paisley towel. I don't like the stiff beige dress that looks like Barbie in a bag.

We have Dawn dolls too, but they're smaller and don't have as many shoes. We name the boy dolls Ken. It's what boy dolls are called unless they're GI Joe. We don't have GI Joe.

The stuffed guinea pigs are called ginnies, and they have adventures where we put them under the sink in the Barbie airplane like stowaways. The captain is a nice man, but he wouldn't want the ginnies in his kitchen. They are slow and silly and sing too much. He doesn't care what Barbie wears.

Your Forever Forever Wife

Each soul emits a stream of light that reaches
all the way to heaven. When two unite in marriage,
their lights flow together, brighter for the union.
—Zohar, *book of Jewish mysticism*

I'm not sure, said Grandma, when Papa
asked in 1932. Certain enough for both of them,
he took her hand that afternoon,
held on fifty-nine years. She squeezed
oranges for juice, baked strudels and chicken,
repeated *The Three Bears* endlessly
to her granddaughters. He gave
three dollars here, five there, spare change
for every rabbi at his door.

In hats and fine shoes they walked together
through department stores and supermarkets,
visited neighbors, made their way to synagogue
every Sabbath morning. When he returned
from the hospital alone after her stroke,
Papa repainted the kitchen
yellow like they had on Eastwood Street.
For the living room he chose eggshell blue,
a color he knew by heart.

Dust settled on the untuned piano.

When Papa died I found a narrow strong box
wedged beneath the dresser.
Inside the cool metal lay a speech, telegrams from Israel,
business cards, a single candle, and near the bottom,
one tiny paper scrap, yellowed tape across the fold.
To my forever forever husband, Grandma had written
one anniversary morning. *Enjoy your breakfast.*
Love, your forever forever wife.

Housewife Microwaved to Death

From a true story in the **Star**

Paula Kelly died in her kitchen.
Microwaves, says her nine-year-old son,
who found her alone. The oven door
hung from a broken hinge and his mom
lay dead on the linoleum, baked
from the inside out like the macaroni casserole
steaming on the counter for supper.

The microwaves passed painlessly
through her clothes, the doctor
explained, cooking her insides, while the skin
remained cool. My mother

knew this could happen.
We were the last on our block
to boil water in a teacup, the last
to reheat soup in three minutes.
She knew. But wouldn't it take longer
than macaroni and cheese
to cook an entire woman?

Click

Kodak instamatic capture.
Black and white of six year-olds.

This one is Lynne, knee-deep in tulips,
hands on hips, with pigtails—
my flower bed, jump rope,
hopscotch, red brick
front porch partner.

We took turns stealing
pieces of each other.
Elbows at our sides,
we squeezed the shutter.
Steady. Breathless.
Sometimes the frame
couldn't contain an arm,
a foot, half a smile.

In this one, she smirks at me.
I've lost her eyes.

Little Girls and Satin

The lingerie lady wears a tape measure around her neck tangled with half-glasses on a chain. She stands all day in a cloud of hairspray, L'Air du Temps and spearmint gum, measuring little girls for first bras while their mothers fidget proudly in the corner.

The lingerie lady reaches up, way up, for a flat white box. She places cotton training bras gently on the counter, one by one. But this little girl has her eye on prettier things. Beneath the glass she sees lace garters, silk camisoles, heart-shaped sachets. She points and looks up. *That one*, she says. Creamy satin.

The lingerie lady shakes her head. *Dear, this one will be fine*. She holds out two white triangles with narrow shoulder straps and a tiny clasp. The child gazes again at the satin, then takes the cotton in her clumsy fingers and walks away.

Where They Sleep

Saturday afternoon
we stand on the lawn, arms full
of carnations and pale roses
from Winn Dixie
as though it's tea time
and we've come to call.

The dead rest in small houses
above-ground in New Orleans,
mausoleums built to hold
entire families, brothers,
wives, children, each
in his own slot

like drawers for buttons
or string, marked with
names and dates,
protected by carved stone doors
that lock.

The cemetery breathes
like a sleeping child
as we arrange bouquets
in green glass vases
and set them on the stoop.

We are not invited in.

No Cross-table Dancing

That's what the sign says
and because it's there
I want to grab the man
at the next table, push
aside my poached eggs
and dance. Dance until
lunch time. Dance
to make the plastic mustard
squeezer jump. Dance
until the napkin holder
and sugar packets
slide across this table
to the floor. That man
sits so quietly behind
his morning paper, with his eggs
and his pressed tan suit. I want
to dance across
the vinyl booth, take him
by the hands
and dance down Main Street.

Simple

Even when I kiss you I know
I could live alone
on clear broth, sourdough, black pepper.
I could bake nut breads like my mother's,
then scatter crumbs for the starlings
who return each March
small and hungry, stunned by snow.

If anything were simple,
I would have turned from these pale streets
long ago, but I'd stored enough salt in the basement
to last two winters, and as autumn held me
in its insulated pockets, I longed to know
if you might be more than accidental. So I stayed

until crocuses cracked the soil,
their purple faces surprising me as always
in late snow. I stayed until you helped the garden
turn to spearmint and potatoes, and even tried to fix
the broken clock in my kitchen where now,
eyes closed near the cooling stove, I kiss you
for dear life, spinning dizzy in the dim light
though I seem to be standing still.

Nickel a Hug

Pearl Kastran Ahnen

I began writing stories when I was seven, later publishing my own one-page neighborhood newspaper. The newspaper abruptly ceased publication one day when my mother discovered a copy and the lead story delved into the family's personal matters. This setback did not discourage me from writing and seeking other avenues to get my work read. Shortly after, I wrote my first poem on a strip of bark and nailed it to my front porch for passers-by to read, hiding nearby to watch them. When they smiled, I smiled. I was addicted. I could not give up writing. Could I give up breathing? I had become a writer.

Now I attempt to create, through my writing, an honest assessment of what I think, cherish and live. I believe my work has practical, common sense values. It's not negotiable. I try to create real people who do not depend on great victories, but on small triumphs of spirit to survive. I'm happiest when I'm writing.

A Promise

Don't put flowers
on my grave, she said.
I want to smell
the daffodils now
while I'm alive.

No gifts on Mother's Day
or my birthday.
Don't need any—
I have everything.

My drawers are overflowing—
scarves, gold earrings,
colognes, cashmere sweaters,
Chanel No. 5.

This morning I drove
out in the country
past fields of
yellow daffodils

turned into an iron gate
walked up a green hill
knelt at her grave.
I kept my promise—
no daffodils, nothing.

Arsenal of Democracy

My mother wanted me to call him Theo Costa. But he wasn't my uncle. He wasn't even related to me. She insisted I call him *Theo* because that was the Greek way of showing *sevas* (respect). He came over to our house on Fridays and Saturdays and helped us make corsages. My father sold flowers on weekends for extra money to buy a used car. Until he got his car, Theo Costa drove him around in his black Dodge. They went to the bars on Woodward Avenue.

Theo Costa usually came over about eight. We knew his knock, three sharp taps, like a woodpecker. One day when we heard his familiar knock, Mama said to me, "Eleni, answer the door." I was at the sink cutting some cardboard to fit the hole in the sole of my right shoe. My father was working at the kitchen table stripping leaves from carnations and roses while my mother snipped fine wire using sharp clippers.

"Good, everybody's working," boomed Theo Costa, coming through the kitchen doorway. He leaned over and pinched my cheek. It hurt. His breath smelled of garlic and old cigars.

"For you, Eleni," he said, handing me a stick of Wrigley's Spearmint. I took the gum and thanked him.

After we finished making the corsages, Mama set out a plate of cheese, olives and bread and two glasses of wine. Papa and Theo drank wine and played cards for an hour. When it was time for them to go, they piled the boxes of flowers in Theo's car.

Theo usually parked on a side street and waited while Papa trudged through the bars on Woodward Avenue peddling his corsages to soldiers and sailors who were with girls. Papa would complain to my mother that some of them called him 4-F or swore at him, but he said he'd just swallow his pride and go on to the next bar.

One Friday while Papa and Theo Costa sat at the kitchen table playing cards and listening to President Roosevelt on the radio, Theo Costa turned to me. "Eleni, you're getting to be a big girl, taller than your Mama. What are you now? Twelve?"

I nodded.

Papa said, "Yes, Eleni—twelve last month. You in Chicago—visiting your brother."

"I have to go again next week. Get someone else for the flowers. Ask Tony."

"Tony, he got jalopy, no run good. Can't get parts. War go on for three years—time President Roosevelt stop it—so we make new cars not tanks here. What does president call Detroit?"

"Arsenal of Democracy," said Theo. But he was looking at me.

Although I was at the sink helping my mother put ribbons on the corsages, I felt his eyes boring into my back. Without even looking, I could see him—his dark hooded eyes, his thin black hair covering a bald spot, his wispy black mustache.

Mama, with her hands deep in a sink full of roses, said, "The kitchen smells like a flower garden."

Theo Costa sniffed, "More like a funeral parlor."

"Oh no!" she said, and made the sign of the cross. I glanced down at my shoes, my toe felt the hole in the right one. Always my mother would hint to Theo Costa that I needed new shoes. She even told him my size.

I wore shoes out fast running up and down twenty-four steps to our flat, walking a mile back and forth to Park School, and playing hopscotch with my best friend, Sally. She had new penny loafers. Her mother had bought them at the shoe store near Eastern Market. Sally even had two shiny pennies in her loafers.

"Money doesn't grow on trees," my mother said. "And if Theo Costa wants to buy you shoes, let him."

My mother always thought the best of Theo Costa. Maybe it was because he had signed papers for Papa to come to America from Greece. Maybe it was because he helped Papa sell flowers. Maybe it was because Theo Costa didn't have a family in Detroit.

Once a month when my mother had saved enough ration stamps to buy some meat, she made a special Sunday dinner for him—roast lamb.

I knew he didn't want to buy me shoes. He never spent any money if he could help it. He wore the same shirt most of the time. He brought his dirty laundry for my mother to wash. The only thing he ever gave me was a stick of gum.

When she'd tell me to show respect, I felt like screaming at her, but I didn't. "*Sevas*, Eleni," she'd say.

All day long, my mother cooked, cleaned, washed and ironed, when she wasn't in church. She spent a lot of time at church answering the phone for the priest and writing letters.

Most of the mothers who had sons in the service couldn't write English, so my mother, who wrote in English and Greek, answered their letters. She read the letters out loud and then listened while they told her what to reply. My mother enjoyed writing letters. Besides doing a good deed, she also heard all the gossip—usually it was about sons who had gambled away all their pay, or others who had fallen in love with foreign girls and wanted to marry them—bring them back to Michigan.

My mother wrote cheerful letters, encouraging them to take care of themselves and have respect for their officers—*Sevas*.

Her handwriting was perfect. Her teachers had taught her the Palmer method. She tried to teach me. I filled page after page in my notebook with looped "o's" but they never looked like hers. She said it was because I was left-handed and I held my pencil wrong. Once after I had finished six pages, I showed them to her.

I knew she was pleased because she let me eat a piece of *feta* before supper. She stood at the sink washing the knife she had used to cut the cheese.

"Soon you'll learn to write Palmer. You're learning a lot of things. You're twelve, a big girl."

"Don't say that. That's what he says."

"He? What do you mean *he*? Are you talking about Theo Costa? Shame. He helps us. Your Papa had nothing when he came to America to marry me. Theo got him a job at Dodge Main. Be nice to him."

"No! I won't be. He's a fat old man, smells of cigars and—and he's not my uncle."

"Hush—Eleni. So he's not a true uncle. He is your Papa's friend."

"I'm sorry." I stared a long time at her. I felt sick, but it wasn't the feta. It felt like I had been on the roller coaster too long at Edgewater Park. My mother said God would punish me for my bad thoughts. But our nice old priest, who smelled of holy incense, said that God doesn't punish children. Jesus loves all the children; they are innocent lambs.

Although it was Friday, Theo Costa didn't come to our house. He was in Chicago. Papa played solitaire at the kitchen table while I finished tying ribbons on the roses. Mama was in the bedroom—mad because Papa was going out with Tony to sell flowers. She didn't like Tony—called him a bum because he didn't work, just lived off of relief, and yet he owned a car.

"Let's play gin, Eleni," said Papa. He shuffled the cards.

"I don't want to play cards." I didn't even want to listen to the Lone Ranger on the radio. Instead, I went to the kitchen window and pulled up the shade. I stared at the alley.

It was May, still light out. If I squinted I could see to the other end. I was squinting when I heard a loud voice. It was my mother yelling from the bedroom. "So you're going with that bum in his wreck, risking your life. He lets the state support him and you work hard and still no car—and for what?

Papa yelled back. "You know for what—to send money to my Mama in the old country, hiding in a cellar. You know I pray that the Nazis don't kill her. And yes, by God, someday I buy a car, like Costa's." He slammed his fist on the table, spilling the wine from his glass, staining the white tablecloth.

That was when Mama walked into the kitchen. She didn't say a word. Just stood there, tight-lipped, wiping away tears of anger with the back of her hand.

Finally Papa said, "What's the use?" and raised his hands.

He pushed his chair away from the table, took his glass of wine, and went into the parlor. He paced back and forth. When he heard the sound of a car's horn, he grabbed the boxes of flowers, raced out of the flat without saying goodbye.

I looked out the window and watched Papa climb into the car and throw the flower boxes in the back seat.

My mother yelled, "Eleni. Get ready for bed. Tomorrow we're going to the market."

"The street lights aren't on yet. Can't I stay up?"

"To bed, Eleni, this instant." She pushed past me into my bedroom and turned down the sheet. "To bed." She was now leaning against the bedroom door jamb, her arms folded across her chest. I started to think, Eastern market, and near the market was the shoe store where Sally had bought her penny loafers. Maybe, maybe—I got into bed.

"Goodnight, Mama."

"Goodnight, Eleni." She glanced at my rag doll beside me. "You're getting too old for dolls. Go to sleep," she said, closing the door.

My bedroom was dark. I couldn't hear what my mother was doing. Maybe writing letters, or looking out the kitchen window. Sometimes I'd stare out my bedroom window; that's what my mother called day dreaming.

Now in bed, I held my doll tight and looked out the window watching the car lights until I got sleepy. That night, I dreamed Papa surprised me with a new pair of shoes, penny loafers, with new pennies in them. In my dream, I wore my new shoes to church. When the priest saw me, he stopped the service and announced to all, "Eleni, our little lamb, is wearing new penny loafers."

The next day, Saturday, we took the Baker streetcar to Eastern Market. It was a big market, much bigger than anything on Chene Street, where we lived. There were farmers shouting, "Tomatoes, lettuce, potatoes, cucumbers," from the tailgates of their trucks.

Whenever we went, there were crowds of people elbowing each other to get at the vegetables and fruit in the stalls. But my mother didn't fight the crowds. She always went to three farmers she knew who had saved her their best. This time she bought string beans, potatoes, tomatoes and onions for Theo Costa's favorite meal. Before we went to the butcher's, we walked past the shoe store. I stopped and pressed my nose against the glass and stared at my penny loafers.

"Come, let's go," she said. "Not today."

My mother spent all day Sunday cooking. That afternoon, Theo Costa came over, later than usual. "Something smells good," he said strolling into the kitchen. "Ah, and how is Eleni?" He pinched my cheek and for a moment his hand lingered on my face. I jerked away. He smoothed the black hairs over his bald spot and reached in his pocket for a stick of gum. "For you."

"Thank you," I said. I frowned.

"Eleni," Mama scolded in a voice that carried worry. But she didn't want to dampen Theo's spirits, so with a bright smile she opened the oven door from which came the unequaled smell of a roast simmering in lemon and oregano. "See? I have your favorite—lamb."

"Good," he said and glanced at me. I stared at his shoes, the same brown scuffed up oxfords I had seen a month ago through the kitchen window after Mama and I had finished the supper dishes. I was looking into the alley where I saw a man wearing those shoes standing in a dark doorway with a woman.

I couldn't see what they were doing, but when he turned to walk away, he was buttoning his pants and I saw his face. It was Theo Costa. I never told my mother, who was at the kitchen table writing letters. I never told anyone. Somehow I knew it was something I shouldn't talk about.

Now he said, "Where's your Papa, Eleni?"

"In the parlor."

Mama said, "Eleni, put some glasses and the wine on the tray, take them in the parlor for Papa and Theo."

"Yes, Mama." I followed him into the parlor and watched as Papa put down his copy of the *Greek Tribune* and looked over his glasses at us. "Ah, Costa, welcome back. Sit, sit." Papa stood and offered him his favorite chair while he moved to the old sofa. Theo Costa settled back in the chair and pretended to listen to Papa, all the while leafing through the *Greek Tribune*. Finally Papa said, "Your brother—how is he?"

"Good, good. He's making money in his restaurant. War or no war, people got to eat."

He folded the paper in his lap and reached into his breast pocket for his cigar, bit off its tip, licked the cigar, and touched a match to it.

He leaned back in Papa's chair and puffed, pursing his lips this way and that way as the smoke circled around his head.

I stood next to Papa, holding the tray with the wine and glasses. Theo Costa looked up at me. "Some wine please?"

Papa said, "Yes, pour us wine—child."

"She's not a child, old friend. She's a young woman."

"Right. Where do years go?"

I placed the tray on the end table, poured the wine and served them. When I started for the kitchen, Theo Costa grabbed my hand. "Wait, Eleni." I freed my hand from his. He sipped from his wine glass, smoothed his black mustache. "Your Mama says you need new shoes. Penny loafers? She's got the ration stamp —tomorrow we go to store—you and me—and I'll buy the shoes. Yes?"

I stood there and waited a long time, not saying a word.

"Well, Eleni?" Papa said.

Theo Costa smiled. "Cat's got your tongue, Eleni?"

"Answer Theo Costa. Show *sevas*," Papa said.

"Yes, Papa."

Theo Costa drained his glass. He glanced at me with a look that made my face burn. He said, "Tomorrow, I buy you penny loafers. Yes, Eleni?"

I looked down at him, sitting in Papa's chair, a circle of smoke around his head, his cigar in his stained hand.

"No. I don't need shoes. Thank you, Theo," I said, showing respect. And I picked up the tray and walked back to the kitchen.

Dr. *YiaYia*

I'm the only kid on the block who wears a garlic clove on a string around her neck underneath her red flannel underwear. It's a secret *pharmaco*, one of my Grandmother *YiaYia's* remedies. Most of the time, the garlic keeps me from catching cold.

When I do catch cold, *YiaYia* slathers warm flannel cloths with camphor oil and plasters them on my neck and chest. She ladles hot chicken soup into a bowl. While I sip soup, water boils in the tea kettle. She pours the tea, honey and lemon into a china cup and stirs in a tablespoon of Papa's whiskey. "Drink," she orders.

Later my head spinning, I stagger to bed knowing in my heart of hearts, I'll be cured by morning. My grandmother is a healer. All the neighbors call her Dr. *YiaYia*.

Tucked in pockets in her long black wool dress are her cures—a silver spoon for nosebleeds, a glass marble for the evil eye, a raw onion for baldness, a candle for backaches, garlic for colds. In emergencies, *YiaYia* uses her black kerchief as a tourniquet.

She teaches me the cures one by one. "Learn," she says.

I'm home from school when *YiaYia* falls, hanging curtains. Before the ambulance comes, I kneel beside her, all elbows and knees, kiss her veined hands, her wrinkled cheeks. Although she assures me, I pray and cross myself—touch the garlic dangling from my neck—and search her pockets for the cure.

Swing Shift at Dodge Main

Two policemen pulled up in a squad car, their tires squealing—it's not that I didn't see them coming. I was the one who called them, right after I telephoned my Mom who was working on the swing shift at Dodge Main. Her job is helping the war effort, she said. Why did I call the police? It was about my brother, Mike. He was gone, and so was the car. Mom was on her way, but the police got to our flat first. From the kitchen window, I could see the squad car come to a stop in the alley. I could see one policeman climb out of the car, pick up a hubcap lying in the yard and pitch it aside. All right, I thought. So they're here. What do I tell them? And what was taking Mom so long?

I went back to my work in the kitchen—plunging the butcher knife into the pumpkin and making the slashes for the pyramid eyes. The one bare light bulb overhead made the ceiling dance like galaxies. I was hoping soon we could paint over the silver stars sparkling on the blue ceiling left over from the last tenant. For now we had to live with them.

We had been in this flat six months, ever since my father left us. He packed up after a big fight. I heard it all, even though I tried to shut out the shouts by putting my hands over my ears. It was about money, or the lack of it. It was about gambling and it was about women.

It started when my father lost another paycheck at the Detroit Race Track betting on gray horses. They were his favorite. Sometimes he'd win, not often, but sometimes. The last thing my Mom said to my father was that she wanted the Ford.

"Over my dead body," he said. "Besides, you can't drive."

"I'll learn. Mike will teach me."

"That's a laugh."

"You heard me. The car is staying."

"What the hell, take the damn car. It will be wrecked in no time with Mike driving it."

"Shut up. I hate you. Get out of here. Go to your whores."

This arguing has been going on for a long time. As long as I can remember. I'm fourteen and I can remember way back. Although my name is Margaret, my Dad called me Peggy. He named me after his sister, Margaret (Peggy) Murphy, who lived in Dublin. He said I have her black

Irish hair, and her green eyes.

My brother Mike said my long black straight hair was witch's hair. "Why don't you dress up as a witch for Halloween, instead of Snow White? Why wait for Halloween? You should dress up like a witch every day." He didn't start saying mean things to me until after our father left. That's when Mike changed.

Now he was gone, and today—Halloween—was his sixteenth birthday. When I glanced out the window, the policemen were walking to our back door. I could see the sun trying to sneak through low-hanging clouds. Looked like rain.

I held the butcher knife over the pumpkin for another stab at it. It was a sharp knife, but I was being careful. Yesterday Mom had it sharpened by the knife-sharpening man who drove through alleys in his old truck, ringing his bell and shouting, "Knives, scissors, knives, scissors." Mike had his Boy Scout knife sharpened, too.

Last night when Mom went to work, Mike was listening to Edward R. Murrow and the war news, which was coming from London. Mom was a riveter at Dodge Main, working on airplanes. She didn't tell us much about her work. It was hush, hush. "A loose lip can sink a ship." That's what she told us. She got the job the day after the Japanese bombed Pearl Harbor, about two years ago. My Dad worked on the line at Ford's during the day. Sometimes at night when my mother was at work, my Dad left the house. I could hear him, although he tried to be quiet. I could hear the Ford starting. He always managed to get back before my mother came home in the morning.

When Dad left us for good, Mom sat us down in the living room and told us that, since we weren't kids, we could take care of ourselves. It wasn't as if she was gone all day. We were given strict orders, to stay at home, not let anyone in the house, and lock the doors.

We did all right—that is until last night, when Mike took off. I had been in my room but I could hear the radio. He had it on loud. I poked my head out of my room and said, "Turn the radio down. I want to get some sleep."

Without warning, Mike screamed, "Shut up! I hate you! I never want to see you again." Then he sprinted into the hallway and ran into his bedroom slamming the door behind him. Glancing back toward the closed door, expecting to see Mike come after me with his scout knife, I ran into my room, closed the door and put a chair behind it. He was weird, I thought. I was unsure of what my next move ought to be, but most of all I was angry with myself for letting Mike get to me.

It was quiet for a while. I couldn't sleep, what with thinking about Mike and his temper and besides, I didn't want to have those dreams. Somehow I must have slept because it was early morning when I got up. It seemed strange. I don't know why, but it didn't seem like an ordinary Saturday.

Mike was usually the first one to get up. I was surprised when I didn't hear any noise in the kitchen. Maybe he was sleeping in, sleeping off his bad temper, since today was his birthday and Halloween. He was going to be the Lone Ranger. When he tried on his costume the other day and put on the mask, I kept touching it, because he looked so strange and he kept saying, "Quit it, Witch."

When I didn't see Mike in the kitchen, I thought I'd better look in his room, even though he had a "No Trespassing" sign on it. I pushed open the door to his room and snapped on the light switch. Two bare ceiling bulbs illuminated the empty room. His bed hadn't been slept in.

Where did he go? I wondered.

Before I called Mom at work, I went outside, and the Ford was gone. Then I did a dumb thing. I went looking for him from one end of the block to the other, half running, half walking, calling his name.

When I finally called Mom, she was angry with me. And at the same time I felt her anger, I also sensed her relief. Strange, but I suspected that she had wanted Mike to run away. That was her way to express concern from opposite sides. What had Mike said to me last night? He'd used the exact words my mother had used when my father left. She had said, "I hate you! I never want to see you again."

After my Dad left, my Mom would say to Mike, "You're just like your no-good father." After a while, Mike began to change. He had accidents. Then he had bigger ones. And I changed, too. I had dreams that I wished would go away. They weren't nightmares, just dreams of getting lost in a forest or drowning in the depths of a lake. And I didn't want to think about the forest or the bottom of a lake. So I drew, pictures of tress in a forest and swans on a lake.

The point that I wanted to make was this: that my dreams were conceptions, not unlike Mike's accidents, walking in front of traffic, cutting himself with his scout knife.

I glanced at the sharp knife I held in my hand. I looked at the pumpkin I was carving. I heard the policemen on the porch before they knocked and I opened the door. The taller, heavier one introduced himself and his partner, whipped out a notebook and began asking me questions. No, I didn't know when Mike left. No, he didn't do anything unusual last night.

I didn't tell them about Mike's accidents. I didn't tell them about the fires. The first time it had been in a closet. We got it in time and no one said anything. The second time they had to lead us out of that house because of the smoke. That's when we moved to this flat. Smoke does funny things to your voice. I sounded strange when I thanked the firemen. I had stood and watched myself lose things and now realized that houses burn and that you must think of what you want to save before they do.

My bedroom in the flat was small, but I had a window looking out on the street. Mike's room was in the back, and his window looked out on an alley. I put some of my drawings on my bedroom wall violets, roses and dandelions.

I was going to be an artist when I grew up. My Dad said I looked like an artist. Mike said I looked like Prince Valiant in the comics. But Mike always said things like that.

Mike's bedroom door with the "No Trespassing, Wild Dog, Keep Out, Danger, Explosives" signs plastered all over it didn't bother me; I would go in anyway. One wall of his room was covered with pictures of airplanes. The other wall was covered with pictures of cars, mostly Fords.

He couldn't decide what he wanted to be when he grew up... a pilot or a car mechanic. He had a big picture of the Enola Gay. He made a scale model of the plane and put it on his dresser. I had helped him with that model.

In the old house, Mike had a snapshot I had taken of him, my Dad and Mom. They were standing by our Ford, smiling. Mike had his hand on the car as if to say, "This car is mine, all mine." That picture was something we lost in the fire.

Now Mom was not smiling when she burst into the kitchen. After questioning my Mom, taking more notes, the policemen left, first assuring us that they would get back to us as soon as they heard something. In the meantime, we had to wait.

It was three hours later when we got the word. Mike had flipped over the Ford at seventy miles per and then landed side-up in a creek on Belle Isle. He had not spun out on a stretch of highway in Detroit. No, he had lost it on a secluded area of the island, no picnickers in sight—no other car on the dirt road or near the creek.

At Receiving Hospital, the doctor said to Mike, "Son, you shouldn't be alive."

The impact must have knocked something out of his head, but all we could see was the cut on his forehead. He had totaled the car and been given fourteen stitches over his right eye. It's a good thing that was all it was. The doctors kept Mike in the hospital several days for "observation" since it was a head injury and because he had "lost" a day. So he missed a week of school.

What concerned me was the memory thing. Why one day? The last thing Mike remembered was listening to Edward R. Murrow on the radio.

What happened after that was a blank—the accident, everything. Maybe that day will come back, the doctor said.

What happened to me after that was even stranger. No I didn't lose a day, I lost my dreams. It happened that night when Mom went to work the swing shift at Dodge Main. Mike was in the hospital, and I was home alone.

Detroit's Best Coney Island

George watched the girl sitting at the counter. He'd been doing that for the last ten minutes. Musn't stare, he thought. That's no way to treat a customer. He turned away from her, leaned on the counter and looked out the window at Michigan Avenue. Cars cruised by. How many times had he counted cars on a slow night at the diner? How many times had he dreamed about owning one? Maybe a Cadillac. Might as well dream big. This was Detroit wasn't it, the motor city?

That girl interested him. How could he be expected to take care of the diner when he was concentrating on her? Not that she was good looking, because she wasn't. It was something else about her. Thin, with washed out blond hair, plain, you might say. It must be her eyes, blue, but more than blue, misty, sad. She wore a simple print dress, pink and green. Why did she look scared?

It was a warm evening and she was the only customer in the diner. So George watched her shake salt onto the fries, squirt mustard on the hot dogs. She ordered three of them, jumbo fries and a large Coke. She ate like a truck driver, already two of the hot dogs had disappeared and most of the fries. But why did she look so scared? A leather brief case lay on her lap.

He might as well talk to her, thought George. They were alone in the diner. "Good, eh?" he asked, in his thick Greek accent. "My Theo Gus, excuse, I mean Uncle Gus, he make best coney island in Detroit."

The girl's huge blue eyes opened wide, "Yes," she said. "The hot dogs are good."

But why did she sound so scared? They were alone in the diner, but he wouldn't harm her. Maybe he could reassure her, take her mind off her fears. She must be afraid of something, George thought.

He said, "We also got best view in Detroit. Michigan Avenue—all the big cars drive by."

And lighting the street was the bright harvest moon. The diner had a southern exposure. All through the summer, George had sat at the cash register, taking in the sun, refusing to think about Theo Gus's obsession. Now he glanced around the diner he knew so well—six stools at the counter, three tables with bent wood chairs pushed against the dingy gray wall. George breathed in the mixed smells— onions, chili and stale smoke.

The store, a narrow, high ceiling structure, was squeezed in between two office buildings. Above the register was an old sign—"Detroit's Best Coney Island."

George moved from the cash register to the counter and wiped it with a rag. Tall and athletic looking, George came to Detroit three years ago from his Greek village. When he was seventeen, George's mother died. His only living relative, Theo Gus, sent money for him to come to Detroit.

He worked side-by-side with Theo Gus at the diner every day and went to school at night. It left him little time for anything else. Occasionally Theo Gus would take George to a dance in the basement hall of the Greek church down the block. The dance was free. Theo Gus avoided activities that cost money.

"Save your money, George," his uncle would say. "Money is king."

Then George would reply. "Money not everything. People important."

George frowned thinking back to the conversations and how they would always end. Theo Gus would spit on the floor.

"Phtew-w, that for people!"

Then the diner door slamming shut pulled George back from his reverie. He turned as Theo Gus barged in.

"Oh, hi, Theo Gus," George said.

The short, stocky man ignored the greeting and instead bombarded George with a volley of questions.

"George, you lock back door? Did dishwasher leave? Coffee urn clean?"

"Yes, yes."

"Good." Theo Gus glanced at his watch. "Time to close up."

He turned his gaze to the girl. "George, you give lady check?"

"Yes."

She looked up. "I'm sorry. . .but, I can't pay. I don't have any money."

"What you say?" Theo Gus snatched the check from the counter. "You owe $8.32 lady. You eat my hot dogs, now you pay or I call police."

"But. . .but," she began.

"No buts, lady, pay, now."

"Let her talk, Theo Gus."

Now the girl was crying. George offered her his handkerchief. The girl crying, the hissing and whining of the old refrigerator, all came together for George. He swallowed, there was a bitter taste in his mouth. Wasn't this America?;Wasn't this where good things happened? He had suffered through a childhood filled with hardship in Greece, to face an even worse adolescence here in America, America where good things happened.

The girl had stopped crying. She folded his handkerchief and gave it back to him. "Thank you. Someone stole my purse, and my wallet."

"What?" George asked.

Now he listened while the girl told her story. She had come into Detroit by bus from northern Michigan. She hadn't eaten all day. She was hungry, tired from the long ride. Before she looked for a restaurant, she put her suitcase into one of those lockers at the bus station. A young man came up from behind her and grabbed the suitcase before she could shut the locker door. Another one snatched her purse. It happened so fast, for a moment she thought it was all a dream. Then she screamed, cried for help. Although there were people in the bus station, no one came to her aid. She ran to the ticket clerk. He called the police.

"The police told me out-of-towners were easy targets for purse snatchers. They wrote everything down. I was so angry, so frightened..."

"And then what?" George asked.

"I just stood there. All my money, my suitcase gone." Her lips trembled. "I'm an artist. All I have left is my paint case." She showed George her case.

"I can pay for the food, I mean—" She did not look at Gus.

"Sort of a trade."

Gus gasped. "What you take me for? I call police, for sure—you-you street woman!"

At that instant an outrageous image formed in George's mind: himself decades from now, an old man, like his Theo Gus

"Theo Gus, no, listen to her."

"Listen to a street tramp, no!" He pushed the cash register shut and picked up the phone, rapidly dialed.

"Please, I didn't mean that," she began. "I came to Detroit because I have a new job here. I'm an artist, and I can paint you a new sign—for my meal. That's the trade I mean." She pointed to the old sign over the cash register.

"No. I call police."

"Theo Gus, give her a break."

"Who give me break?"

"People."

"You make me crazy—all the time with people. Shut up."

He slammed the phone down onto the counter.

"Yes, Theo," George said. He glanced at his uncle and the girl. Outside it was dark now, and the street deserted.

"Yes!" George could not control the anger coming up in him.

"No, Theo!" He slammed his fist on the counter. "No! Three years! Three years. Always—yes, Theo. Three years."

George's anger would not let him finish. He reached in his pocket and pulled out a ten dollar bill and threw it at his uncle. "Enough money to pay her bill?"

The old man did not move. "For all I do for you George, you treat me—like this? Shame."

They stared at each other.

"And here," said George, turning to the girl while she wiped her red-rimmed eyes with the back of her hand.

"Here's forty dollars; you paint new sign, eh?"

"Don't give whore—money," Theo Gus said.

"I can't take your money," the girl said.

"Yes, please take, get room tonight. Good hotel. No rough place. And Miss Artist, make us big sign, say..."Detroit's Best Coney Island."

Nickel A Hug

I found it in the attic after her funeral—leather worn, silver clasp tarnished. Inside were four nickels and two dimes. Nickel a hug, dime a kiss.

Years ago, I saw that coin purse the first time I met her, my grandmother from the old country. She swept into our lives on the arm of Papa one raw October afternoon, her hair tucked under a black wool kerchief, her big body squeezed into a long black *foosta*, skirt. Later, while we sat in the parlor, her green eyes, large, like the rest of her, were fixed on me, as if they might pull me toward her. "*Cot-seh*," (sit), she said. I giggled. That made my brother laugh.

"Stop it." Mama scolded. "Sit with *YiaYia* (grandma). Hug her. Papa gave her money for you."

YiaYia nodded and lifted the hem of her dress. I gaped as she peeled back layers of black underskirts, rummaged in a deep pocket and pulled out her coin purse. She dug into it and offered me a nickel.

I shook my head, backed away. I didn't want to hug this stranger—even for a nickel. That was when my brother shoved me. I fell against her, caught the smell of pine tar soap from her hair. "No?" She snapped shut the silver clasp.

"I'll give you two hugs," said my brother, palm open. While they embraced, I looked away.

Now I sit in the attic—her coin purse in my lap—finger the nickels and ache for her hug.

The Gypsy

Tula was a prisoner during the winter of 1926. Day after day the Chicago wind piled snow in high drifts and made it impossible for her to leave the flat. Isolated from the world, her only contact was with books. Reading had become very important to her. She lost herself in books, spending hours huddled next to the kitchen stove, reading.

She had discovered an old copy of Homer's *Odyssey* in a pile of Papa's books. While Vasso and Angel did their homework, she sat by the stove and read. Her favorite passage in the *Odyssey* was about freedom. She even wrote it in her Friendship Book—"Freedom is neither wine nor a sweet maid—it's but a scornful, lonely song the wind has taken." She wondered, had Papa tried to find freedom in a wine bottle?

Tula was a prisoner in this flat. And the flat seemed to have been designed to catch every draft. Although the kitchen was cozy and warm from the stove, the other rooms were cold. She went to bed in a cold room, got up in a cold room. And pouring hot water from the kettle into the tub behind the stove to wash were how the days began for her.

As for Andreas, when on rare occasions he was home for supper, hearing him joke and tease her sisters and tell stories, you wouldn't know he had a care in the world, unless you studied his eyes. Since the morning of their quarrel last summer, his eyes were never happy. She remembered his words, "Why aren't you pregnant? We've been married for more than a year. What's the matter with you?"

After their quarrel, he didn't spend much time in the flat. He'd leave in the early hours and return late in the evening. He said it was his work that kept him away.

The weeks before Christmas were the busiest for him at the candy store. Hand-dipped chocolates had to be made; walnuts, cherries and raisins marked with their special swirl. Boxes had to be packed and shipped. Mr. Pappas demanded perfection in this time-consuming work. There was only one way to make the candies—by hand. Thousands of miniature works of art were created by Andreas. Each chocolate was placed in a fluted cup and nestled into a box circled with a red or green satin ribbon.

After the holidays, there was a lull at the candy store, but Andreas did not come home. After work, he went to the coffeehouse, or the back room of the grocery, where men gathered to play cards. One Sunday in late January, when the weather had turned colder Andreas managed to come home early. An eerie gray had seeped into the sky and lasted all afternoon, slowly fading into the east when night came.

"Too cold to snow," Andreas said. He sat with Mama and the sisters around the stove in the kitchen. Tula read to them from *Alice in Wonderland,* another book from the library. This was the last one from the pile she had borrowed. The books—worn, thumbed volumes—traveled from one sister to another. It was Tula who ventured out every two weeks, trudging through the snow drifts to return the books.

Now as Tula finished the last page of *Alice in Wonderland*, Reni said, "Read *Little Women* please, Tula?"

"Haven't you had enough?" Andreas asked.

"No, never," Reni said. She grabbed the book from a pile beside her and gave it to Tula.

"I'm getting hoarse," Tula said. "Vasso, why don't you read for a while?" She placed the book in her lap.

"Me?" I can't read aloud," Vasso said.

"Never mind, I'll read," Andreas said. He took the book from Vasso. He was not a reader of books. And try as Tula would, she could not persuade him to read a book. But to ensure his welcome in the reading circle, he brought the sisters candy. "All right, *Little Women* it is," he said. He leafed through the book. "Say, this story reminds me of you girls." Though a smile was playing around his mouth, his eyes were hard.

The girls grew silent and uneasy. Tula said, "But—you don't like to read."

"I changed my mind. I can change it, can't I? You're tired of reading, and the girls want to hear another story."

Tula wondered what he was up to. Since their argument, he had become distant. If she couldn't give him babies, maybe he'd leave her. She didn't care. She'd be better off if he left her. Didn't her mother tell her she had to save the family? Would having babies save the family? Where would the baby sleep in this crowded flat? In a drawer of the old dresser?

As days passed Tula noticed her mother and Thea Sophie in deep conversation while they crocheted. What where they talking about? She sensed it was about her. The two women would laugh like school girls sharing a secret but when Tula came in sight, they'd stop and exchange knowing glances. While the chicken soup simmered on the back of the stove, or the coffee pot perked, they whispered secrets.

Thea Sophie had all the answers, Tula thought. Didn't she teach her mother how to bake Easter bread, and how to crochet lace runners for the altar? Didn't she introduce Mama into the world of the gypsies and fortune telling? And if Mama knew it was wrong to consult the gypsy and have her palm read, wrong in the eyes of the church, she could not discipline herself not to visit the gypsy. Tula knew that the best Mama could do was to make sure the old priest did not find out.

One day when she got back from the library, Tula hung her scarf and coat on the hall tree and pulled off her galoshes. "Mmmmm, that bread and coffee smell good."

"Sit down, you must be cold. I'll pour you some coffee," Mama said.

"We have something to tell you," Sophie said. She could not contain herself, she was so excited. "Yes, we have good news, child."

"She's not a child, Sophie. She's a married woman. Some day, God willing ,she'll be a mother. Tula we're taking you to the gypsy. She'll cure you, and you'll have plenty of babies."

The next day, a reluctant Tula, plodded behind Mama and Thea Sophie as they walked into the gypsy stoe and faced an old gypsy woman. A scarlet scarf was wrapped around her gray hair. Smiling red lips revealed yellow teeth. A long black velvet robe covered her ample body while a gold cord circled her thick waist. As she drew closer to her, Tula's nostrils began to sting from the odor coming from the gypsy. She backed away and brushed her damp hair away from her face and looked down at her new shoes, now ruined. Mama also stared at the shoes. "Why didn't you wear your galoshes? Look what you've done to your new shoes. Do you think money grows on trees?" Mama asked in Greek.

"I. . .I forgot. You rushed too much. I didn't want to come here in the first place."

The gypsy came between them. "So this is the childless woman? Why, she is no more than a child herself. How old are you dearie?"

"Sixteen."

"So young?" There must be a strong curse on you, and it might take more than one visit to lift it. I will need a gold coin to start." Her palm went up as she spoke.

Mama reached into her coat pocket for a black-bordered handkerchief knotted at one end. She undid the knot and gave the gypsy the coin. The old woman bit into it and smiled. With a forward motion of her hand she drew Tula near. "Sit down, my dear." Three wooden chairs and a green velvet arm chair surrounded a table. Tula glanced at the maroon-colored walls which seemed to have been painted years ago, judging from the condition of the chipped paint. The storefront windows were draped in purple velvet.

The gypsy took a crystal ball and a deck of cards from a shelf. She looked at Mama and Thea Sophie who stood in a bewildered huddle. "Sit, sit," she commanded. "Did you collect the remains of the male fluid from their sheets? Did you snip hair from the husband's head, a fingernail from the wife? And dust from beneath their bed?"

Mama nodded and produced a folded black-bordered handkerchief. She unfolded it.

"Good," the gypsy said. "We're almost ready." She reached over and took the handkerchief from Mama, spit three times into it, knotted it and slipped it under the crystal ball. The gold coin she dropped into her bosom. She shuffled the cards and revealed an ace of spade.

"An ace of spade," she whispered and frowned at Tula, who was sandwiched between Mama and Thea Sophie. And now, as if in a dream, she watched the old gypsy take two candles and light them. The candle smoke, the gypsy's odor made Tula close her eyes for an instant. "Open your eyes!" the gypsy screamed. "I can't remove the curse if I can't see into your soul." She touched Tula's arm. Tula shuddered.

The gypsy took her hand away. She smiled, her thin red lips slanted at an angle across her lined face. She whispered, "The curse must be lifted." She went into her ritual, gazing into the crystal ball, shuffling the cards, chanting, while the rain beat against the store windows.

"Yes, it will be lifted!" Thea Sophie said, caught up in the ritual. She had not spoken since they had come into the store. The gypsy cried, "Hush, hush!" She slumped over the table, her fingers circling the globe. Suddenly a wrenching moan, swallowed in the depths of her throat, came from her. She closed her eyes and in a blind touch-search of the crystal ball, she pressed her red lips on the crystal. She said, "I see a baby. Yes, a baby."

The gypsy opened her eyes, "Put your hands on the crystal," she commanded Tula.

Powerless to call a halt to this madness, Tula's hands came up to clasp the crystal ball. It was as if she were in a trance; the stench of the gypsy overwhelmed her. Perhaps if she were still, very still, the old woman would back away, and this feeling would pass. The gypsy put her veined hands over Tula's for a moment. Suddenly she reached over and unfastened a button on Tula's dress. She worked fast, her fingers flying across the row of buttons. All the buttons unfastened, she reached down and touched Tula's firm breasts, squeezing, feeling, caressing. Tula startled, shivered. She looked down at her exposed breasts. The gypsy said, "These breasts are too small for a baby to suck."

With a start Tula's head came up and she screamed. "No. No!" she flew at the gypsy like a savage, clawing at the old woman's face. "Don't you put your filthy hands on me!"

"Bitch!" the gypsy cried and slapped Tula hard across her face. Suddenly all became confusion. Tula drew in her breath and pushed the old woman. "You're crazy, old woman."

Mama and Thea Sophie watched in horror. "No, Tula, don't," Mama said in Greek. "She means well. She will help you."

"I don't want that old bat touching me, ever!"

And with a sweep of her hand, Tula sent the crystal ball crashing to the floor. With her fist, she punched the gypsy in the stomach and ran out the door.

Outside at last, she ran back to the flat disgusted with herself—all the while wanting to curse, wanting to scream, knowing what had frightened her so, made her run from the gypsy, run from Andreas, run from the flat. In her mind she saw her baby sleeping in a drawer in the old dresser, another prisoner in this flat.

Tender Freight

Gerry Tamm

For me, words have been the key to a mysterious universe. They open doors to places I have never been, my eyes to things I have never seen. The most intriguing journeys I have taken are into poems. I begin with sensory images that lure me to my soul where I explore the universe of my experience to discover the meaning of these images. Enticed by the melody of words, I am carried by the beat of the music. When I read a poem, I must take this trip more than once. The first visit is a whirlwind tour, the landscape seen through the windows of a tour bus. To visit at my leisure, to linger in the hidden recesses, to discover the mysteries, to come upon myself, this is the pleasure of a poem. When I write, the trip is more arduous for I must find my own way and am often surprised by the destination. Revisiting is the difficult task of *re-visioning* until I get it right.

Magic Eye

I didn't even know it was there, that rectangle of color like a Jackson Pollack, tucked in with the ads for All-Bright Carpet Cleaning and Belvedere Construction, between afternoon and prime time in the weekly TV Book, which I consult daily for the evening's diversions, until I idly picked up *The Magic Eye* from my daughter's coffee table and following instructions saw the ocean of fish and the air filled with hummingbirds in glorious 3-D, then went on to the complexity of the western hemisphere emerging from a sea of faces, dinosaurs from a primeval forest, and my eyes opened to a parallel universe like the ones St. Paul saw through a glass darkly and Captain Kirk took us to time after time after time, where no man has gone before, in the star ship Enterprise, a realm of God and angels, new life forms and infinite possibilities, visible only when we look through the screen of distracting sensations in our humdrum lives and focus through the printed colors so that forms emerge layer by layer until we can reach no farther, a vision that can be lost in a blink if we are distracted by the page, and the wonder of it all exists even when we do not open the book.

The Year We Found Each Other

In that year of possibilities,
we defied gravity with cream

whipped in icy bowls, held upside down
above our heads. Tears flowed and laughter

floated like the cream atop the steaming
coffee laced with sugar and old Bushmills.

Friends came and went. We wondered where we'd be
next year. We celebrated every moment

with whipping cream moustaches, cool froth
on the tips of our noses, and burned our lips

on the bittersweet liquid below.

Masquerade

Unmasked
I came to you
and we danced
out of control
toward the stars
our bodies fused
in step with
the pulse
of the universe
our lungs
unaccustomed
to the thinness
of the air.
I breathed
the hope of
the ionosphere
but you looked down
grasped the tentacles
of earth and I
gave in to gravity
and followed
trailing sparks
put on my mask
and we continued
the dance, our feet
on solid ground.

Dancin'

My husband hates it
when I lead,
no problem when
we dance free.
He feels the rhythm
moves with it
takes me with him.
But we do rounds now
choreography to
  rumbas
  waltzes
  cha-chas
  two-steps
  tangos and jive.
A man who doesn't like
  to be told
  to conform
  to count steps,
who likes to
  show off
  improvise
has learned the
  two-step
  vine
  and hitch,
  the scissors
  diamond turn
  and twinkle,
loves the showy
  serpiente
  peek-a-boo chase
but when it comes to
the solo left-turning box,
he fakes it.

Saving Face

I tap the jewel-blue bottle against my palm,
releasing a pool of milky fluid,

dip my middle finger as I was taught by the Avon lady
who applied the coat of color that masked my girlish blush
like the greasepaint of my theater days transformed me—
look at your skin! you have no pores!—to my future face,
and frightened my three-year-old son to tears,

listen to the morning news declare the Japanese prime minister
disturbed at losing face in trade talks with our robust young president
and sympathize, recalling the recent evening when I turned on
the wrong burner, then scorched the pot under the watchful
eyes of my son, and thought, this is the first sign,
not the wrinkles my gallant husband sought to prevent with
an array of potions for my birthday ten years earlier, which
I promptly returned for cash to waste on some frippery;

I caress the life-restoring fluid into each crevice of the face
I sometimes do not recognize when I glimpse it unawares
or face it in the bathroom mirror before my morning rites.

Remodelling the Chelsea

We're good at greeting mornings, you and I.
We felt the earth rock when we came together.
We shared our heartache when we said goodbye
to youthful hopes and dreams no matter whether
yielded willingly or stripped away
by time. We looked for backroads where we found
surprises—remember the Rhododendron Cafe?—
and sometimes stumbled covering new ground.
Now we watch for each new year's discoveries,
the trillium in spring on the way to the lake
and when fall comes the scarlet maple trees.
We treasure memories that time can't take:
Devonshire tea at the Chelsea, savoring a scone
with cream and jam, another pleasure gone.

Morning Coffee

Dawn's flimsy curtains drape the mirrored bay
as wisps of steam rise from my sun-hued cup.

I sip the bitter brew in silence, straining
through the mists of memory for sounds

long gone—the rush of falling water from
the stony dam replaced with concrete pylons—

children's squeals, splashing at the water's
edge or chasing through the brush now cleared—

laughter carried on the evening breeze
as boys forsake their frogging for the girls—

and the sweet tones of the trumpet wailing
through the night, plaintive sound, captured

in that overgrown deserted silence
in the hollow, only I can hear.

Gentle Night

Sometimes when I lie in bed in my darkened room, with only the glow of my bedside lamp impressing itself on the darkness, I see you sitting near me brushing your long gray hair, and I am a child, warm and loved, tucked into my featherbed.

Your beautiful hair reaches to your knees. How do you wrap it so tightly that by daylight it seems to be just a knot at the back of your head? I like the night.

You read to me. Strange stories in a strange tongue. I don't understand the words but somehow I know what they mean. The Book is sacred. I understand and live in the grace of God. I like God.

After you finish this nightly ritual, you turn off the light and climb into bed with me and I sleep snuggled up with you and the featherbed. I don't need a teddy bear. Dolls are for daytime. Nights are dark and warm and snuggly. Some people are afraid of the dark. I'm not.

I wake up alone again. Someday I'm going to wake up first and find out when you get up. It must be dark, before the sun gets up. It's cozy here in bed and the house smells of good things, coffee and something baking. I hear a rhythmic flop, flop, flop. I know it's Sunday. If I hurry, I can watch you toss the noodles up and let them fall on the floured board. You make noodles every Sunday for our soup. Chicken soup, of course, because we always have chicken on Sunday. Sunday is my favorite day.

I'm lonesome when you go to church. I know my mother's here but she's sleeping. I have only my dolls to talk to and the hour you are gone seems like days. Sometimes I get into trouble but it's not because I'm bad. I remember when I spilled the baby powder. It was an accident. I thought I cleaned it up. I rubbed it into the wood until it hardly showed. Of course that part looked lighter so I added some more and then some more until the rest of the table looked the same. I don't remember how it got on the plants. Maybe because it smelled so good. Anyway, you sure got after my mother when you got home. She was supposed to take care of me. I can take care of myself.

I like to play under the dining room table. It's like a big cave with a tree in the middle. The chairs are the rest of the forest. I sit leaning against the trunk and feel the grooves of the roots at the bottom. They feel like animal paws, a great big bear. When the Sunday tablecloth is on I can only see out if I bend way down almost to the floor. You can't see me.

When dinner is over and dishes are done, everyone gathers around the table to play cards. Not my mother. She goes out. I get to sit on your lap and help play your cards. I like the king and queen best. They're pretty.

Sometimes you talk in another language and then you all laugh. I don't know what's so funny. Sometimes I say things and you laugh too. I like the way everyone laughs and has fun. I laugh too.

You give me a sip of your wine. It's sour but I like it. I want more. Mother always says not to give me any. I'm glad you do. Sometimes I get dizzy like I do when I twirl round and round in my favorite dress and the skirt swirls up and my pants show. Mother doesn't like that dress. You gave it to me. I love you.

Your lap feels good. Your body feels warm. My head feels funny. I'm sleepy.

I wake up alone.

At Gramma's House

There was a picture in her living room:
a little girl, her yellow dress falling
to the toes of her patent leather

Mary Janes as she bends to pick
a flower, Shirley Temple curls bobbing
at her neck, a Peter Pan collar.

Seeing it again, the child is me.
I had a dress just like it: soft, cotton
voile gathered to a shoulder yoke,

a white pique collar piped in brown,
flowers embroidered at the front. Or was it
a photo I remember, black and white,

the dress tinted yellow at the colorist's whim?
Did I see the flour tracked from room
to room by the wheels of my stroller

from Gramma's flour bin—just my height—
on the pantry door, or did I picture it
from the story often told, from the

tangle of mismatched synapses like
those that lead my mother door to door
in her past, through long abandoned rooms?

Coat

One day I tried on Mother's coat
and when I looked into the mirror
I saw my mother there.

Her redolence imbued each thread
impervious to the many years
spent stored in cedared air.

What shall I do with Mother's coat,
the image staring from my mirror
a coat I cannot wear?

No Graves to Tend

We came to bury her last sister in that
drought-caked soil, the long parched grass crisp
beneath our feet, autumn sun ablaze.

The ritual done, we wander from the graveside
to search for stones of years passed by. We find
her father, and the mother she knew for only

six years, and with them John the hired man,
embraced in death, no family of his own,
and the tiny stone of little Thomas, gone

before her birth, brother nonetheless.
She knew him from the picnics on the stones,
from tending graves and leaving flowers in honor

of their memories. I mourn because
I have no graves to tend. I do not know
where my dearest ones are buried.

Requiem for Sister Bernadette

She was wearing purple when we left.
Luscious lilac. Violet beads and bangles
at her ears competed with the sparkle
in her eyes, her smile, her soft gray hair.
Her silky blouse fell in graceful folds
from her wasted shoulders.

She went with us to mass
that morning at the villa, then to dinner
where she picked at food but relished the good
wishes of her sisters. She was radiant
with unearthly light of faith and courage.
The year before, she glowed in candlelight
reflected by the snowy linens, sparkling
crystal, as we savored Christmas strawberries
with Grand Marnier served by a bowing waiter
dressed in black and white, reminiscent
of the habits of her younger days.

Northern lights ignited the sky the night
we buried her. A burst of red more startling
than a roman candle crowned the shimmering
bands of green along the earth where she
lies clothed in matching green reflecting her
triumph over death.

There Is a Season

From a sea of white, I watch
the buds release their tender freight
through a fever haze.

Sinking, sinking into the
maelstrom of sheets, sucked
into my rotting lungs,

I feel my body shrinking.
This is what it is to die:
to see the spring unfurl its green

and not to care, and not to care.

Lanternes

TEN O'CLOCK
Black
steaming
coffee-laced
conversation
flows.

HANDLE WITH CARE
Words,
weapons
keenly-honed
aimed precisely
cut.

FOUR O'CLOCK
Tea,
amber,
shared friendship
in a china
cup.

UNSTRUNG
pearls
scatter
a necklace
broken, falling
tears.

Circle of Friends

They do not count the passing years, nor see
the signs of aging brushed away like dusty
cobwebs, like the pain of life's disappointments.

They hide from each other the cruelties they suffer
like the cards they play. There's never a whisper
of unpleasantry to disturb their chats of travel,

clothes and food and treasures and surrogate
accomplishments, their children's, husbands'.
They weep behind closed doors.

A Time to Dance

As lemmings to the sea, we fled our barefoot girlhood
rushing to the shoe store for our first high heels.

We tottered to the floor mirror, admired the curve
of our legs, posed coyly side to side, and

did not see the tilt of our hips nor feel
the strain in our backs. Like the little mermaid,

we wanted to dance so badly that we accepted the pain
and this deformity. What we gave up that day

was the reverberation of the earth beneath
our feet, our dance of freedom, all that wildness,

to cramp our toes into an ill-formed space designed
for sexual attraction, starry-eyed by the

illusion of the perfect love, the perfect man.
Of course the choice was ours. We were not

girl children in China. Our feet
were not bound for the pleasures of men.

When Greek Men Dance

they begin slowly, in a line
arms held high
hands resting on each other's shoulders
heads bowed to watch the steps—
to the right, knee lift
step, knee lift, again
forward, back, side, again
dip forward—again, again
until the pattern is established
and they lift their heads
and their faces glow
as the strings
grow louder and faster
and the beat of their feet
vibrates up their legs
tilts their hips
as they twist and dip
to the strum of the strings
heads thrown back now
and the floor resonates
carries the rhythm
to our feet as we watch
and can barely keep still
and our bodies sway
and our hands come together
keeping the beat
with the thud of their feet
and the throb of the strings
faster and faster
until the room explodes
and we can no longer
contain ourselves
and we leap to our feet
in wild celebration.

Daughters of Athena

Lost
in the labyrinth
of Mykonos,
I wish for Ariadne's string
to draw me through
the intricate design
of walkways leading
to the sea
and think of
the Byzantine women
painting portraits
with their needles
while the beauty of Greece
crumbled about them
and of Penelope
at her loom
weaving and picking
to ward off suitors
while Odysseus
dallied with Calypso.
Men build
their monuments of rock
while women
with a single thread
bind millenia.

A Straight and Fragile Line

Sandy Gerling

I had a flashlight hidden under my bed when I was a child, to read stories and encyclopedias way past my bedtime.

Writing.

I make oatmeal in the morning and feel moved by the inherent possibility of this simple act.

Writing means.

I get on an airplane seeing all the people around me and know that incredible mysteries lie in each one of them.

Writing means this.

I come home to find another one of my shoes chewed up by Molly and wonder how it would be if she could tell her story.

Writing means this to.

I hear stories of others or hear myself tell an old one, and I believe in the endlessness of where words can take me.

Writing means this to me.

A Straight and Fragile Line

My mother's back was balsa wood. I stepped on every
crack in the sidewalk and knew she cried in her sleep.

On the wood around the window screen I have scribbled
I love me, I love me. A mosquito on the mesh loved me too.

Whirligigs line my path to the lake, two seeds embedded
in the fall by a straight and fragile line.

He was still sleeping, unaware of my breath in his ear
as I rose from a bed of rumpled sheets and drove to New Orleans.

Satin slips are obsolete, silk panties run twenty-five
dollars a pair, and linen tablecloths are a bitch to iron.

I have held a hot poker next to my face, but it slipped
from my hand when everyone left the room.

Storyteller

Coming through the darkness is a woman holding a flashlight. Centuries ago, she would have held a lantern, but these days it's a battery powered gizmo. I'd like to say she is a myth in the making, a story unfolding, which she is, but there is never-ending distraction that keeps me from telling it the way she wants it to be told. So she fades in and out. Sometimes she is very distinct, wearing jeans and a long blue sweater. Her Reeboks traipse through leaves in the fall, and her bare feet kick water at me from the shore of Lake Huron when it's summer. At other times she is vague, an anxiety, or a foreboding anticipation. She mocks my lack of concentration with a smile that is wicked and taunting, as if she is the one doing this to me, and not the other way around. She may as well use a cattle prod for what she does to me with no more than a look. I am a rabbit caught in the headlights of an oncoming car, afraid to go forward, afraid to go back, but knowing the impact is inevitable as the car comes barreling at me. She walks through the places I have yet to penetrate, the places I have turned my back on, and when I'm not looking she can inject a sense of doubt, and a lack of understanding deeper than any real person has ever done. She is imagination and destruction, desire and hopelessness. I have bent my body in response to her demands and wailed when she was absent. To continue the story is what she needs and though she tells me I need it too, warning me that it is essential if I am to go on living, I still call her names. I still don't believe she is real.

Making of a Cradle

I just can't help it, I must howl often. I must howl at the full moon and at the crescents in every phase, and in the mornings when the moon is fading and why stop there, I must howl at the sun in its rising and at midday and at the reds and oranges of its passing into night. Coming up over a hill I see the sun halfway hidden in the clouds and shafts of light are breaking through and I howl, my mouth like a big circle, an orange, a mandala, a wedding ring and sound pours out. Sound from the vibrations of the first cells that breathed, the voices of those who have been forgotten, and from the woman who was me, who had been buried and is now unearthed. She was almost out of breathe and about to give up. She couldn't help it, no more could she scratch at the hard places trying to break through, her fingers caked with blood.

At night when I was a child, I'd put on my pajamas and brush my teeth while my parents watched TV and read dime store novels during the commercials, and when I wanted to say goodnight, they'd tell me to wait until the commercial came on or when the chapter was finished. So I'd go to bed and tuck myself in. And wait. I fell asleep to the sound of Johnny Carson's voice sending me into the dreamtime. I couldn't help but turn the howl inside out while I slept. I didn't know that howling inside breaks many things. The spine grows crooked from sound going the wrong way. Juices that naturally absorb toxins gradually diminish and are ineffective over time.

Since I began to howl, I stalk the sounding of life like a beast, making up my being as I go. I have howled through the room of abandonment and disconnection. At first the noise was deafening from so many others crying and wailing, but they calmed down upon hearing the animal in me show itself to the animal in them. I moved on and into the room of cleansing, showering myself until the skin shone, and only new cells remained on the outside. Toweling myself off and dressing, I felt prepared for what was ahead.

I howl into the abyss, but fear there will be nowhere else to go once I am there. For years I have avoided this place, pleading an unpreparedness in being able to withstand the fall, but now I hear the sound of my howl as it comes up to greet me, somehow familiar and comforting, catching me as I fall into darkness. Not because I want to, but because it seems I have no other choice, I lean back to let this darkness and the sound of my voice cradle me. I am surprised to find that it is enough.

Buried Desire

I want to bury myself like a mummy. Who would ever know I had such desires? I want to know death in this way, while I wait for a carefully selected crew to unearth and bring me out into the warm summer sun, unwinding the strips of cloth from my body. After having done that they would leave, as expected, unable to contain what had just happened. Who would ever guess that it is me who steals wine from the neighbor's refrigerator, only to return it a week later, just to create a stir, some excitement in this boring neighborhood where the houses sit too close to each other and someone calls the police for a dog barking or leaves burning? Who would guess that when I drop the kids off at school, I drive to Canada and watch women dance? I'd prefer men, but catch as catch can, and in the daytime it's only women who will take off their clothes and bare their flesh. Some of them are good, and I can tell they are in their bodies, and others are off somewhere else. I know that look.

Once, my father went as a stone to a Halloween party. My mother had made a costume for him out of burlap. When he got to the party, he curled up in a ball in the corner and had my mother put the costume over him and there he stayed for the entire night. He won first prize. For months after, he would smile like a man in possession of some precious gem. Who would guess that he hit me for no reason, told me what a waste I was? Or that my mother hated to touch me for reasons of her own that died when she did? The trouble is, that these things go on living in me.

I tried to run away when I was not quite two, my hunch is that even then I knew something was amiss. My mother was called to the door, roused from a sound sleep by a motorist asking if she knew who's child was wandering around in the middle of Gratiot Avenue. I had come close to being run over by all six lanes of traffic, as I made my toddler's dash across the highway. By then someone had taken me to the side of the road, and though I do not remember any of this, I can feel it at times. The standstill of terror when I'm in the middle of somewhere or something and I am sure there is an invisible force coming at me, never sure whether or not this force will stop before it runs me over. It's like feeling I'm always just around the corner from being hit by a bus, even if I'm standing in the bathroom brushing my teeth.

After that, I was tied to the kitchen table with a rope when my mother napped, which was daily and for hours. Don't ask me how I can remember this thing at such a tender age. I don't know. Perhaps it was only once. But I do remember another time when I was older and had the chicken pox, and I was tied up again, this time with strips of white sheets around my wrists, with the ends attached to the bed frame, so I wouldn't scratch while I slept. Maybe this let them sleep, but it was the door closing, and the long hours until morning that gave me plenty of time to hate them while I drifted in and out of a fitful sleep. "For your own good," as the saying goes, to keep the scars off of my face. I showed them though, and picked at the scabs during the day, and carry a pock mark on my cheek to this day, to prove to myself that they couldn't stop me from doing anything if I wanted to do it bad enough. For my own good.

These stories are not something you go around telling people. They don't get you anywhere, not that there is anyplace to be gotten, and more than likely you'll hear a quip about how sorry you must be feeling for yourself and how others have had it so much worse. I stop there, though there is more, but like I said, these are not things you can just go around telling people. That is why I'd like to be a stone, or a table, or a lake, and because I can't be any of those things, I have tried to become a bit more realistic. I have found some white sheets and believe me that wasn't easy in this day and age of art nouveaux and deep purple, and have begun to tear them into strips to use for the wrapping of my body.

At some point I'll begin to build myself a box out of plywood, big enough so I can lay inside. There is a longing to hear the sudden sound of the earth as it falls on top of me. I am sure there is a certain insanity to wanting this experience, desiring this, believing it would in some way lead to a breakthrough. Or maybe there is no peace, maybe it just keeps going on, like the days of my childhood, waking every day to the fear, the fear of pain, of bruises, and of words. Some have said none of this ever happened, and I doubt myself, have I made it all up? Who would know that I wanted them all to die, back then, for doing such things, and now, for not believing such things have happened. Those dark times have wrapped themselves around me like an impenetrable veil, and not only on the outside, but within. How can a gentle hand or kind words ever reach the very mitochondria of my being, release the coating around those silken stands of DNA?

But that was a long time ago. Now I only want to be buried. I gave up the happy ever after story that someone would come to my rescue after seeing the profound goodness that was locked up inside of me and coax it out, only to find these places in my soul of unstoppable destruction. Flat and barren landscapes, a wasteland, howling winds that pierce my skin like sewing needles, and no arms to hold me, no trickling streams in which I could purge myself of this terror. People say to me: you are your own worst enemy. It's an old story. I am tired of the repetition. I have pushed a boulder down a mountain and it won't stop. It just keeps going faster and faster and just before impact, I blank out. Again and again, the scene repeats itself, the same boulder, the same mountain, the same blanking out. I'd like to say to these people who tell me this," But you don't know, you don't understand." Instead I nod and say, "I know I am my own worst enemy."

So I keep the enemy a secret and water my plants and feed the family nutritious meals and plan trips to the Caribbean, while I tear sheets into strips and tuck them neatly into a box I have in the back of my closet. There are days when I can say to Hell with it all. I can say, "Lighten up," and I do. I can think positive thoughts and motivate myself to do all sorts of things. But over the last few nights, I have awakened with my heart pounding, certain I have slipped into the madness I have long feared, for I see myself under the earth screaming, running out of air, while above is not a crew, but one person who has thrown down the shovel and is walking away. It is me. I realize that she has desires even more secret than mine, and she is not about to tell me what they are. She has no intention of digging up something that she would like to see stay buried.

The Shifting Earth

Each pilgrim kisses the earth with lips of gratitude, thanking whatever God he believes in as the one who brought him safely to a new world. The old order has crumbled. Water breaking the surface from an underground stream quenches the thirst of squirrels and elk, Canada geese and muskrat in the northern woods of Michigan. A flock of pintails rises to a tremor of distant rumbling. A rare Michigan earthquake has occurred, 3.5 on the Richter scale. The land shifts, settling deeper into itself. Fields and mossy banks of the stream are altered and readjust to the new terrain. "The universe keeps expanding, and there may be more than one universe, maybe even thousands," my son has told me with an air of knowing as if it is a secret no one else knows. His hair falls over his face when he bends over to tie his shoes and I see him leaving, taller and wider across than he is now. "What do you suppose holds all the universes together?" I ask. "They're trying to figure that one out," he says. I ask him the question again, wanting to know what he thinks, not they. He gets it and shrugs, "Who knows? It's a mystery, I guess." Pushing his hair back, I can see that this answer is enough. A box can hold a heart that is only moved with great effort by the owner of the heart. The box is heavy, made of lead and interlocking wires which lead out in every direction attaching themselves to the oddest things. Next to my bed is a black stone that serves as a reminder of all my hurts, the betrayals I have suffered, the chances I have missed. It is smooth on the outside from years of rubbing and though I know it has the potential to be an amulet of destruction, I still hold on, falling asleep with it between my thumb and forefinger. I am used to its soothing feel. Before long I will wear a hole right through the middle, and maybe then I can give it up. Maybe then I'll understand something. The earth has shifted and we are leaving an axis in which we were once familiar. At times when I am dozing, I can see the inside of the earth, red and swollen, cracked and oozing through her many pores. Some are closing, and new ones are being formed, breaking through the surface in places that were once stable. A woman I have never met walks at the edge of the Pacific Ocean, stepping over knotted cords of kelp. She feels a shift in the sand as she walks, it's different than the day before. She wonders as I do, "What is required of me? How do I ever leave behind all these stones I have carried into my heart?"

Eggs

"Stop spreading stories around the neighborhood," Leslie's father told her mother out by the chicken coop. Leslie's mother had been collecting eggs in a stainless steel bowl, leaving each hen with one so she would continue to lay, and was coming down the stairs of the coop. Leslie was watching. Her father had been next to the coop with a machete, hacking at the untamed trumpet vine that threatened to take over the Macintosh tree, until he saw his wife and strode over to her, machete still in hand. Leslie's mother took a step back, he looked wild and unpredictable with the machete in his hand, but it was more than that, it was the familiar look in his eyes no one ever messed with, though the stories Leslie told of the neighbor boy were true. He had done things to her on the evenings he had baby-sat. Leslie's mother nodded and turned her gaze to the bowl, counting twenty-three for the day. A good amount, but too bad, it was one egg short of a dollar. Her fingers touched the tops of the brown shells as she walked toward the house. Leslie looked up from an anthill she was pretending had caught her attention near the back steps, but her mother walked right by, as if she didn't even see her.

"Forget about it now and don't go around the Frasiers anymore," Leslie's mother told her later that day. The neighbors had already stopped speaking to her when they bought their eggs. With a strained expression, they took the cardboard carton of brown eggs nestled safely inside, while Leslie's mother went on about what had happened with the neighbor boy and her daughter. She had expected a sympathetic ear, a siding with her about this awful thing, but the neighbors had known the Frasiers longer and believed none of it. The Frasiers were kind and always had a big summer party in the field behind their house. Their sons played baseball with their sons, slept overnight with their sons, and nothing had ever happened to them. They had stopped talking to Leslie's mother about gardens, hot summer days, crabby children, and the latest triumph of whatever their children had been doing. Leslie's father stayed in the fields or woodshed, silent, tinkering with old motors or things he found along the roadside on trash day. It was more than her mother could bear and she cried while weeding the gardens, wiping the tears away with her soiled hands. It scared Leslie to see her mother like this, so she hid when she saw the bowed head of her mother going toward the flower beds or vegetable garden.

Barred rock hens lined up against the far wall when the girl went into the coop the next morning. It was Leslie's job to feed and water the chickens before she went to school, and when she rose on hot summer days. She had to empty the feed trough and scummy water bottle, and fill them up with fresh water from the hose and mash that was kept in a barrel inside the door. Sometimes it was Leslie and not her mother who collected the eggs. This was her least favorite of chores. No matter how hard she would try, there was always a broken egg in the bowl by the time she set them on the kitchen counter. As she moved through the coop that morning, as every other morning before, their black and white striped bodies huddled together in the far corner. Some scurried through the narrow hole into the chicken run outside. Leslie had always thought they were stupid creatures and on this morning she told them so, while she squirted them with the hose. She quit only when the din of squawking became so loud, she was afraid it might arouse suspicion.

Leslie stayed away from the Frasier's house and played in her back yard among the fruit trees and giant oak, never near the road, in case the oldest Frasier boy was passing by on his bike. There were no new scenes tucked away in her memory of him standing at the bedroom door while the mother and father were out for the evening. No more rubbings against her small body with her face pushed up against the wall or moaning that made her play dead. She got to go to the drive-in with her parents that summer, and even managed to stay awake all the way through most of the second features. In a way, her mother tried to make it better by buying her a special treat while they were at the drive-in. It was always hard to choose between her favorites, a Snickers bar or an orange snow cone.

Submerged like a stone off the isle of remembering, Leslie's mother began to sell her eggs again with friendly chatter, while apologizing, "My daughter made it up you know. I just don't know what I'm going to do with that girl and her overactive imagination." The neighbors nodded and agreed, while talk of the latest crop ripening, or this year's abundance of ragweed invading the flower beds, took up the lack in their previous conversations. Leslie's mother was pleased things seemed to be back to normal and didn't cry anymore. Leslie was relieved too, not only had all the crying scared her, she had begun to think it was something she did wrong to cause her mother's tears. Mother just wasn't the crying type.

A vagueness entered Leslie's life. Darkness made a cocoon around her body, it was as if her body was far away. Her mother complained about the constant stumbling and asked where she had gotten so many bruises. She didn't know. There was a confusion as to what was the truth, after hearing her mother speak to the neighbors in that way, as if nothing had happened, making her doubt her own remembering. At night, just as she was about to drift into sleep, she would be startled into alertness by her heart. It had started to do this funny jig, and though it frightened her, she told no one. She would lay while her heart calmed itself, listening to the sound of cars passing by, or the TV that was on late into the night. After awhile she came to believe that it wasn't a very big deal, and after a longer while, she started to think that maybe she did make it up. Maybe she was the bad one.

In the warmer months, the chickens usually spent a great deal of the day outside in the wire chicken run. That summer, Leslie furthered the chicken's fear of her by inventing a new device of torture. She stood at the far end of the wire run and poked a stick through, scaring them toward the small door that led back into the chicken coop. Then she ran ahead, beating them to the door and blocking it with the stick, which kept them from going back inside where it was safe. This went on for a very long time, until she was breathless from running back and forth. When she was done, she threw the stick against the coop for the final scare, and walked away. She hated herself for doing it, but she couldn't seem to make herself stop.

At a Sunday dinner twenty five years later, Leslie saw an opportunity while her father tinkered in the basement with a weed wacker someone had given to him. Her mother had made a Key Lime pie the day before, according to Leslie's instructions, except for one very important part: the pie had not been refrigerated. Leslie looked with disgust at the results. The pie had turned a dull yellow and was separated from the edge of the crust. There was a thick brown liquid laying in the space where it had separated. "You left it out all night," she accused. Her mother slumped over the table amidst the chicken bones and potato skins. Leslie stood with her hands on her hips, face turning red, "Do you wanna make us sick? Those were raw eggs. You can't leave out raw eggs." She picked up the pie in irritation and swept it off to the kitchen saying, "I was really looking forward to having a Key Lime pie."

The pie slid out of the pie plate easily, merging with coffee grounds, crumpled tin foil and chicken fat. Coming back to the table with a chocolate cake, Leslie looked triumphant. "Good thing I made this cake," she said, handing her mother a generously cut slice, and just as Leslie's mother was about to speak, Leslie interrupted, "Just forget it Ma, you never listen to what I tell you."

Icicles

It had been a long time since she played with icicles. Toby could see them out of the front bay window hanging off the eaves, where she sat inside on a seventies love seat her mother had bought at a garage sale the summer before. They glimmered from the streetlights. One was very long, halfway down to the porch, and the others were catching up.

Toby lived inside with her mother who was a registered nurse. Most times her mother had the day shift, but today she was working afternoons. Toby didn't mind being alone, she was old enough, fourteen, though sometimes she got lonely. When her homework was done and she was tired of the TV, there was nothing to do. She knew she wouldn't be able to go to sleep right away. It had been gray out for days, people wouldn't even look at her in school, and her best friend, Amy, was mad at her about some stupid thing. These things wore on her at this hour. Maybe she could call Vanessa and complain about Amy, but it was 11:20 and she was probably asleep.

She called her mother, even though it was a no-no. If the 'old hag' supervisor was around, her mother would catch hell for getting a personal phone call.

"Hi Ma. There's this huge icicle growing down to the porch. It'll touch pretty soon."

"Well that's nice," her mother said distantly, probably charting, tying things up so she could get home. "Did you do your homework?"

"Yes Ma," Toby answered.

"Isn't it late for you to be up?"

"Yeah, but I can't sleep."

"So this is what you called me for?" Her mother's voice had an edge of irritation to it, and Toby knew she should quit before it was too late. She couldn't help herself.

"When are you coming home?"

"In about an hour, but you should be in bed by then. I don't want to find you up when I get home."

"Yeah, yeah, why do you always have to stay so late? Don't write so much and you could be home earlier."

"Tobeeeeey." Now she was getting mad.

"There's nothing to do around here. I hate it." Toby fingered the lacy curtain that curved around the bay window, pulling at a string she found fraying at the bottom.

"Toby, go to bed," her mother commanded.

"Okay, bye."

She hung up the phone, her hand listless on top of the tan princess phone, yanking hard at the string of the curtain with the other hand, until a piece of the string broke off. She dropped it to the floor, staring out the window at the icicles.

Toby went to the small coat closet and took down a cardboard box bordered in roses and looked inside. A purple scarf. Two pairs of long johns. A zip-out lining to a coat. Old mittens way too small for her hands, and a pair of worn leather gloves of her mothers. She tried on the pair of mittens, and found the edges only came to the bottom of her palms. These mittens were from the sixth grade, before her dad had left. While they still made snowmen together. She tugged at them, pulled until they stretched to cover a fraction of her wrist. She wrapped the purple scarf around her neck. Now for boots. In the back of the closet she found a pair of polyester Muk-luks.

Her dad had called them that. The words were funny and used to make her laugh. Everything was reminding her of her father tonight, when all she wanted to do was go outside and break off an icicle or two, maybe suck on the end and taste the bitterness of melting snow. How he used to laugh at her when she put these boots on and tramp around shouting, "Muk-luk, Muk-luk, Muk-luk." She would stumble and fall, the boots being much too big. He told her the Eskimos made them from the skin of reindeer, but Toby would have to settle for plastic. Toby told him she didn't mind plastic, because she didn't want to wear anything on her feet that pulled Santa's sleigh. She put on the boots, brushing of dust from the tops of the feet. They fit much better now.

No one knew where he was these days. Her mother had given up trying to get the friend of the court to do anything. It would cost money to track him down to pay support. She told Toby to just forget about him, they could do it on their own now.

For awhile after he moved out, he was in town living in an apartment just a few miles away, and Toby got to see hem every other weekend. He would come in his rusty pick-up truck and she would have to sit on a seat full of Burger King hamburger wrappers and French fry cartons, shoving as many as she could over before she sat down. The floor of the truck was the same, pizza cartons, apple cores, and beer bottles. They would drive off and see a movie or go bowling.

Once, he took her to the Ice Capades at Cobo Hall in Detroit. She had resisted, saying it was too babyish for her to watch *The Little Mermaid*, but it was magical. She had loved the skaters floating over the ice, the spotlights following them in reds and blues, and the music from *The Little Mermaid* filling the place, echoing off the walls making a muffled sound. One of the skaters fell a few times, so it wasn't perfect, but she knew that her dad loved her.

Toby put on her ski jacket and went outside. There were several icicles in addition to the long one that went halfway down to the porch. She broke off two of the smaller ones and threw them against the sidewalk that led from the porch to the garage. The streetlights buzzed an irritating fluorescent sound. She pulled off two more and threw them at one of the lights. They fell way short and landed in the snow bank next to the street.

"Shut up, shut up," she said to the streetlights in a low sharp voice. She wasn't scared to be out so late, but she didn't want any of the neighbors to wake up and tell her to go in, or worse yet, tell her mother she was outside at this hour.

Tears began to trickle down her face and chilled her cheeks when the night air gusted. She wiped them away with her little girl mittens. Toby never cried much, she decided it made her stronger. She felt it was shameful to cry over something no one could do anything about.

"You bastard," she said to her dad, pulling of a larger icicle. She could hit the streetlight if she tried hard enough. She stepped down off the porch and held the icicle in concentration, took a few running steps and let it go. Missed. It landed with a satisfying crash on the street.

A few years before, her father had taken a job in Cincinnati. He said it paid better money and even had health insurance. Toby could never get a straight answer as to what kind of job it was. "It's just a job," he said,

"A nine-to-fiver like any old job." She quit asking him questions about his life. He said he would come up and visit her once a month, but only managed five times, the last time being a year ago when he dropped out of sight. He had to get cheap hotel rooms when he came. He'd always complain about how much it cost him to stay for the whole weekend. Sometimes he would drop her off on Saturday, even though he was supposed to have her until Sunday, so he wouldn't have to pay for another day at the hotel. The last time she saw him, she was annoyed, he wasn't like a dad anymore. She wouldn't go to any of the movies he suggested, or go bowling.

"I hate bowling." She grumbled, her lips in a tight straight line.

"You like bowling," he said, as if he knew everything about her.

This made her even more irritated. "I have always hated bowling. It's you that likes bowling. I want to go to the Gap and look for jeans."

"I'm sorry honey, I just don't have any extra money this month."

"You never have any money. You never do what I want you to do. You never come and see me."

He hardly spoke to her the rest of the weekend. They spent their time watching TV from the room, going out to Big Boys for meals. She hated Big Boys, too. She told him it was for cheapskates. When he dropped her off on Sunday, he told her he wasn't sure when he would be able to make it up again. The new job wasn't working out.

"Why can't you get a job up here?" she asked, kicking the debris on the floor of the truck.

"There's slim pickings everywhere. I wish I could. I wish I could." He was shaking his head, and she realized by the tone of his voice, it was phony, the whole thing was a bunch of lies. He didn't want to come back. She looked at him, and it as if she was looking at a total stranger. No traces of her real dad were left. She got out of the truck, slamming the door, and wouldn't even look back when he called out, "Bye Toby. I'll call you."

"Liar," she yelled, forgetting about the neighbors, and vaulted another icicle at the streetlight, barely missing it this time. He had never called, not that she had expected it, but after awhile her mind had made up stories about him. That he would come back and be her old dad. That maybe he acted the way her did was because he had a brain tumor and everybody knows that brain tumors make a person act crazy. He would come back and explain it all to her, while she would inspect the place on his head where they had cut out the tumor, and then he would take her somewhere. But these were only stories.

"Asshole." Her voice louder. She had been so close.

The large one was the only one left. Saved the best for last. She broke it off carefully and held it gently in her hands. What a lovely thing it was, clear and glistening. She could see all the way through it. There were waves of yellow and white going throughout it. Every so often there were blue streaks that shone in the light with a brighter glint. They looked like cracks. She wished she could show it to someone. Maybe she should save it for her mom to see, but she'd be too tired and get angry at her for not being asleep. It was much too big to put in the freezer to save for tomorrow.

It was all because of him that things were the way they were. "You are so beautiful," Toby whispered to the icicle. Without thinking about it, she took quick aim and threw it, with all the hate and mixed up feelings she had inside, right at the streetlight , screaming, "I hate you, I hate you."

It flew straight into the windshield of the Pultz's old Chevy parked across the street and shattered not only the icicle, but the windshield, and whatever resolve she had left. Her jaw tightened. With balled up fists, she fell to the ground pounding the crusty snow.

"I missed. That was my last chance. It's no fair."

The sobs broke loose inside, the ones stuck there for a long time. She tried to make them stop, but they felt good in a way. She let the snot dribble down to her lips. A few times she wiped her nose on the jacket sleeve, leaving moist trails across her arm.

After awhile, she got up and glanced around, relieved that no one was out. She supposed she'd be in trouble over the windshield, since she knew she would never be able to lie. She had promised herself a long time ago that she'd never, ever lie, even if it was hard. It was worse to lie.

One of the Muk-luks had fallen off and snow had crept inside. She stepped into the boot not noticing it was full of snow, and went into the house. As she pulled off the boots, she saw all the snow inside one of them and realized that her sock was wet. After scraping the snow into the laundry tub with her fingers, she tipped the boot upside-down over the heat register to dry, and lay the wet sock next to the boot. Tipping the boot upside-down was something her dad used to do. She put everything else back into the closet, except for the damp, too-small mittens, which she also laid on top of the heat register. As she was locking up and turning off the lights, she knew there was one more thing she had to do before she went to bed. Striding over to the drying boot, she turned it upright and set it back onto the register to dry. "There," she said to herself, sure that the boot would dry much faster her way. Which it did.

A New Ritual

New Year's Eve. Lisa decided to make bread. It had been so long that her ten year old son couldn't remember her ever doing it. She started to explain the process and he seemed excited to help. They were alone. She could have gone somewhere, she had been invited out by a girlfriend, but then Alex would have had to stay with a babysitter. Soon, he would be spending his New Year's Eve with friends, like her eldest child.

They went to the grocery store to buy the yeast. She had enough flour, oil, salt, and sugar. It was white flour and though she had debated with herself before they left for the store whether or not she should buy whole wheat flour, she decided against it. Alex wouldn't eat it. No tinted bread for him, stubborn kid, and if they were going to spend all the time it took to make bread, she wanted him at least to eat it.

There were only a few people in the store getting last minute party supplies. Chips, beer, and soda filled their shopping carts. She and Alex were standing in the express line with two packages of yeast, one for each loaf, when one of her neighbors walked by. Janice was a pain, always trying to set up dates, telling her she needed to get out more, get laid once in awhile. Maybe it was true but Lisa disliked her crassness, the thick make-up she always wore, even in the morning, the short skirts, and her never-ending nosiness. Janice saw the yeast in her hand and asked what she was doing, and without waiting for an answer, went on, aren't you going out tonight, I am, he's a hot number, yum, yum, can't wait to see him, do you believe it, I've run my pantyhose and now I have to get another pair, they won't be on long anyway, I don't know why I'm even bothering, I hope I'm not going to be late to meet him.

"I'm making bread tonight," Lisa answered when it was obvious Janice still wanted to know what was going on.

"Bread? Really? What a Susy Homemaker you are. Did you get a breadmaker for Christmas or something?" Janice asked.

"No, I didn't get a breadmaker." Alex was getting fidgety, and the line was finally moving a little faster. They were almost to the conveyer belt. "Hey look, I gotta go."

Janice shrugged and left, clacking in her high heels to another express lane. They were next in line when she started to feel a familiar sinking from the lump in the middle of her chest as it traveled down, spreading like strangling tentacles of a morning glory vine while it covered everything in sight. She put the yeast on the conveyer belt. Once they are in a garden, it's almost impossible to get them out, and nothing else can live under their demanding need for space. Her son started giggling, rolling his eyes when Janice was out of sight behind the magazine racks, batteries, and doo-dads. He shook her out of these dark musings of morning glories. She paid for the yeast and they headed home.

Lisa showed Alex the bread secrets. The same ones her mother had taught her, and a few she had discovered on her own. She told him that before he was born, she used to make bread almost every week. She told him how the water couldn't be too hot or the yeast would die, and if the water was too cold the yeast wouldn't activate at all, both things leading to flat bread. She showed him the exact temperature and let him dissolve the yeast. She showed him how to knead properly, folding over the dough from the opposite side of where it had been just pressed down, so all areas were kneaded evenly. How the kneading must be done over and over for a good ten minutes, without the hands sticking, adding more flour until the hands felt loose and the dough pliable. She showed him how she could tell that the bread had been kneaded enough by poking two fingers into the dough and when the dough popped up, that would mean it was done. She let him knead and add the flour, letting him poke the bread from time to time, watching the change in consistency until at last it was perfect and the dough popped right up, leaving no fingerprints. She let him grease the dough so it would rise without cracking and set it in the bowl.

"That's it," she said, "except to lay a kitchen towel over it while it rises."

"What does that do?" he asked.

"It's called 'veiling the bowl.' My mother said it was to keep the bread a secret until it was time for it to be seen," she explained.

"Well that sure makes a lot of sense."

"Well I don't care, I liked secrets and my mother made it sound special."

"What's so special, the yeast is supposed to make it rise. It still doesn't make any sense."

"Well, you don't always do things that make sense, some things don't make any sense no matter how hard you try to figure them out. Why don't you just trust me on this one," she lectured. He moaned and went off to build Lego spaceships, while she remembered the smell of bread baking, walking by the oven feeling its warmth, the glow of the colonial light that had hung from the ceiling where she grew up, the nubby brown glass casting off soft light globes onto the walls and cupboards.

Lisa's mother had always complained about the poor light in their kitchen. "Good for nothing," she would grumble when she tried to read a new recipe. "I don't know what ever possessed your father to put in such a worthless light." But Lisa had always liked how that worthless light made everything look fuzzy and soft. Not so dirty and run down. She remembered times she would lean against the cupboard, still too young to do much of the kneading, and how she would watch her mother's hands and the shadows her ample body would cast against the wall. And later, when she brought over friends, especially boys, and they would wind up in the kitchen, eating and talking. She had felt comfortable there.

It was good to remember, she thought, not all things can be put down. She had pretended when she got the divorce that many things of the past did not matter any more. The light, the arms and hands doing something useful, the waiting for the bread to rise, getting a sense of slow time. The way the breeze would come in through the kitchen window and spread the aroma through the whole house, and not just in the house of her childhood, but in all the places she had baked bread. The first tiny apartment they had in Royal Oak, the house they rented on Willowmere, in Mt. Clemens, the first home they had bought in Troy, with the biggest kitchen and the best light, and now this new home. The one she had made on her own. It had a small kitchen but a good use of space, with big windows out to the backyard that let in the afternoon light. These things she did not want to leave behind, and there were these new things she wanted to keep.

After an hour, she showed him how to punch down the bread and form the loaves. They had decided to make three small loaves, instead of two large ones, to fit in the toaster better. The bread had to rise another hour and it rose nicely, with no large air bubbles on the surface she would have to pop with a toothpick before baking. The smell of it baking filled her with memories of easier times, of times when she and her ex-husband still got along, when they still had kind words for each other, a time when she felt she had purpose. Just before midnight, Lisa removed the bread from the oven. She had barely taken the loaves from the pans when she cut her son and herself a thick slice. The bread was so hot they could hardly handle it. She took the crusty end, her favorite part. They spread gobs of whipped butter on the slices and sat down at the kitchen table to eat them as it turned into the new year, not even bothering to watch the apple go down on Times Square, like they did every year on T.V. It was quiet for a few moments and she enjoyed this new way of bringing in the New Year. Then there was a gunshot and someone started to bang a pot a few doors away. The noisy celebrators had begun, while they chewed and swallowed. The bread's crust was gold and crispy, and the inside had a fluffy rich taste.

"Hey," she said between bites, "now this is the way to do it, eat your way into the New Year, so long as you don't eat too much of your way in, or someone will have to pry you out from under the table."

"Ma, you are so weird," Alex laughed. "And you're even funny sometimes."

"Oh yeah." She set her bread down on the table and began to tickle him until he begged for mercy.

Gunshots, firecrackers, and banging pots filled the night air as they settled back in to finish up their bread.

"I wish we had fireworks or something," he said.

"Well, we do have a pot or two if I recall," and they both raced together to the cupboard where the pots were, grabbed one and a wooden spoon from the drawer and began banging. He started to run through the house and she tried to yell over the din to stop, you'll knock something over, you're too wild.

"Oh ma, lighten up," he shouted at her. She yelled back that at least they should go outside if he wanted to run around. He tore out the front door. She wanted to do the same, run around and scream, but she stopped herself. She realized that she wanted her son to trust a little, believe in the need for the veiling of the bread, while she was having a hard time trusting she could have fun on New Year's Eve.

Lisa stood at the front door, banging her pot but stopped, when a car pulled up in front of Janice's house across the street. Janice got out and holding the door open, screamed something to her date, while he screamed back. From the vantage point of the porch, she could see Janice as she reached back into the car trying to hit her date and he, blocking the blow with his arm. She backed out of the car, and screamed once more before she slammed the door. The car screeched off, Janice's eyes never leaving it, until the car turned the corner and was gone. Alex had gone on banging the whole time.

Janice looked over and called out sarcastically, "My, oh my, aren't we having a good time."

He yelled back, "We sure are."

Janice turned at her front door and looked across once more and then slipped into the house. Lisa watched for a long time, but Janice never turned on a single light.

"Happy New Year, Happy New Year," Alex yelled.

She was looking at Janice's dark house, thinking about new rituals and old things to be left behind, and about some old things she should keep and remember. It was because of the new year, she supposed, it was the time to make promises to herself. Lisa realized that Janice, with all it looked like she had, dates, places to go, excitement, was racing along after the same dream she had. Find a man, and all will be well. It was an old thing, like a garden full of morning glories blooming the same blossom, killing the variety of the garden, its different colors, shapes, and smells. It was forgetting to trust in the bread to rise, always needing to peek under the towel to see if it was really happening as it should. These old habits had to go, but how, she wanted companionship, she missed sharing her bed with someone.

Her son came up on the porch, exhausted, panting, with hot, red cheeks.

"Can we do this every year?" he asked.

She told him sure, we can try. They went in the house, and the aroma of bread was still present and seemed to have penetrated every room. As she was putting away the pots and wooden spoons, she thought that she had to do more than try. There were new rituals she could create. He wanted another piece of bread and she held the smooth top of the loaf gently while slicing, as if it would crush under the weight of her hand. There was no one to tell her how to do it. There was no "one" way. She began to wrap the bread in tin foil, but her hands were trembling. She stopped and looked at them, as if for the first time.

"I can make it up as I go," she said to her hands.

"What?" her son said with a mouthful of bread.

"I said, I can make it up as I go."

"Oh." He was pulling off the crust in one long piece, trying not to break it.

She leaned against the counter and watched until he was finished. He wasn't tired, but she insisted on bed. In a few minutes, the house was quiet, he was more tired than he thought. Standing at the counter, she let the sounds of the night settle in. Finding comfort in the stillness, she unwrapped the bread and with a sure hand, sliced off another thick piece for herself.

Fields of Milkweed and Salt

Vivian DeGain

Are we there yet? my daughter asks from the back seat as we drive to my mother's house. *Is it ready yet?* my son calls, impatient in the kitchen, as he smells the cooling cake. *When is it going to be done?* We stick our fingers into the fluffy pink frosting, whirling into waves under the beater.

Is it done yet? We ask ourselves, our editor, each other. Is this line, this poem, finished, the story finally there? This collection, is it a real representation of what we want to say? Is it just a slice in time or will the frames we've captured remain individual, universal? For generations?

When does revision end, and the glow of birth burn in our cheeks?

When did it begin? With conception? With labor? With the baby's first cry of life, or with the first urge within our bodies?

I am the little girl in the back seat. I am the voice, the question, the journey, and the route. I am my mother, waiting for me to arrive. I am the bowl, the beaters, the kitchen and the waves. I am the body of work, and the work is a walk down Woodward Avenue, feeling all boldness and sway.

Grandma's Brass

The reeds of her voice, raspy
from years of hollering
across the dry Missouri grass,
hollered louder than the clanking
streetcars in Detroit. The way
she bellowed *Sister* summoned
children seven blocks from home.

Grandma said her back stayed
straight, her hands flexible
from eighty-some years of
planting and pruning, picking
beans and canning beets.
She used a dinner knife
to scrape corn cobs for relish,
an old spoon to pit plums for jam.

She was partly right, maybe just as
lucky at genetics as she was at Bingo.
Shake them up, she clamored at the priest.
You can win real money, she claimed,
if you get number thirty-two in the corner.
Grandma would quote the Bible or claim
the jackpot with the same Southern nonchalance.

Grandma liked to call us *Sister*,
so she could hear her daddy's voice
echo her childhood in her ear.
Sister, he'd said, *There's*
twelve mouths to feed.

She'd turned fourteen
and had a way to earn a living.
She'd learned how to guide
tiny babies into the world,
how to stroke the mother's forehead,
when to tell her to lie still
and when to holler,
Push, breathe, just let the pain
go away from your mind.

When we were children,
Grandma heard our heartaches,
broke our fevers,
and rubbed consolation
deep into our chests. Her medicine
lingered like the smell
of the brown greasy tin.
Wear an old t-shirt, it will stain,
Grandma said as she stroked
the salve on our temples,
across our shoulder blades,
and under our nostrils.
Calling the healing luck to her
she worked in the words
as she worked in the salve.

Remember, Sister, this one thing.
Wherever you go,
you end up there alone.
You've got to walk that lonesome valley.
You've got to walk it by yourself.

Bat

Insomnia hangs from the rafters,
a tiny velvet umbrella
that folds up into itself.
Its eyes, blue glacial ice,
accuse me of sloth,
of being lazy and disorganized.
Like echolocation,
I throw it out and it comes back again,
amplified mosquitoes
that murmur lists of chores and more.

Its pointy ears of silk and fur,
are cupped for sonar,
hear my heart's longings
for a day with nothing to do,
for an afternoon in the park
watching clouds,
or a group of college boys in tight jeans.
Instead of being forty with three kids,
I'm eighteen and have a frisbee,
which I throw into the air.

I hear the saucer whir in the dark overhead.
I feel the whirl by my face.
It's silky and black,
a small soaring boomerang the size of my hand.
Wings of webbed skin,
its fingers brush a line across my lips
and sail in the moonlight.

Sleep would be a blessing,
but the bat circles in the night.
It glides through the murky fog
and sniffs the smells of salt and blood
and nags and nags to feed on me.

Rearranging My House

My toes wriggle in the moss
as I walk to reach the front porch steps.
The wooden railing peels green paint
and the chimney billows clouds of steam.
After my hysterectomy,
my house grows visibly.

I walk into the foyer. It opens into a labyrinth
of halls, staircases, attic, cellar.
Intuition says to go right
to follow the cool bumpy plaster.
The ceiling slants like an Escher,
to a door too small to go anywhere.

Another room, I say turning the doorknob.
I've found another room.

I wade in, and the room sprouts.
I dig through waist-high scraps
of emerald zigzag,
velvet, satin, silk
and discover a tapestry of two brown bears
unraveling into ribbons of purple sheen.
I find Aunt Anne's mink pillbox hat,
and sort through bunches of lace and cultured pearls.

Rearranging the mess, I find
a chipped porcelain colander,
some dried red rose petals,
and a natural wicker basket
holding three smiling salmon.

The salmon chant through the wicker:
A strong woman can always find
another egg in her skirts.
She can spawn the roe in her pocket,
or if too early to develop,
she can poach them for breakfast.
They are good for the stockpot,
no waste, no waste.

Frames of Malcolm

My father, Malcolm, was a painter,
passionate, when he could find the time
to push oils into seascapes, as big as the wall.

A tool-and-die maker the rest of the time,
he worked as a boring mill operator.
Malcolm said it was boring, the most boring job on earth.

Malcolm made us stilts of wood.
His rubber band guns
were the best anyone had ever seen.
And Malcolm was a drunk.

He drank highballs of Nat King Cole, Mitch Miller,
and Harry Belafonte.
He taught us all the words as the old phonograph sang.

Most of the time Malcolm worked midnights.
But always first at my bedside,
he sang *Stardust* right on key.

His fingers dusted my back, star light,
to quiet little girl worries.
I always knew,
some morning soon, he'd live somewhere else.

The Cyclist

You bet your legs will knot and scream,
he says, grinning and perfectly serious.
Your nose runs,
shoulders bang and cry.
Your fingers melt the handle grips
and your butt burns in the saddle.
His butt is dynamite.

Practicing his visual imagery, he sees
200 miles in twenty-four hours. Rain or shine,
he knows May weather on Belle Isle.

He tastes the walleye wind drafting the Detroit River.
His hip joints know if it will help or hurt his time.
Long before they met, he rode the marathon.

The tension in his calves and thighs
needs to push the pedals against the pavement,
a fury that needs skinny wheels,
spokes that sing his sweat,
a song of long muscles and bones.

He counts rotations of the left foot, the down strokes,
cycles of breath, revolutions per minute, target heart rate.
The composition is pedal and dance.
He calls it cadence.

He dances better than she.
His brain counts in a different meter,
but she fell in love with his determination.
She wanted to oil
his skinny wheels, his alloy frame.
Alloy, he says, *is lighter than plastic, stronger than steel.*

Her visual imagery sees him balance babies
in his timing, raise them with his gluteal conviction
and teach them to ride
smoothly, in the cycle of their marathon
and dream of long country roads,
with climbing hills, fresh black top,
trees on both sides for shade,
and no chasing dogs.

Spring Memory

Real pets don't make good presents for the holidays, I heard on the radio recently. The novelty wears off, they say.

But every spring, I drive past a sign that invites *Free bunnies, for a good home.*

One Easter morning when I was ten, my younger sister, baby brother and I woke up to find something special in our kitchen. Beside our wicker baskets, arranged on the kitchen table as usual, with Sander's chocolate bunnies, jellybeans, and gooey marshmallow chicks sprinkled with yellow sugar, there was a cardboard box under the table.

While we tried to decide which candy to unwrap first, we heard peeping noises and scratching from inside the box. My brother, a toddler, managed to get the lid off the top. It wasn't the puppy we'd been begging for, but the Easter Bunny had left us three fluffy ducklings.

Three baby ducks, in a cardboard box. We squealed with excitement, and scooped up our downy ducks and held them close to our nightgowns. The ducklings shivered and squeaked.

We didn't notice the eyedropper on the table, left no doubt by the Bunny as a hint to feed our duckies. Since Mom and Dad were sleeping in, we helped ourselves to plastic cereal bowls and filled them with milk, water, puffed wheat and malted milk eggs. The duckies pecked at everything, but didn't really eat anything.

By the time Mom and Dad woke up, we had filled our bathtub with lukewarm water. I knew to make the temperature just right, because Mom had taught me how to test bathwater with my elbow.

When Mom and Dad came into the bathroom, they found three kids in their bare feet, and three ducklings happily paddling through bubblebath.

Like the kid logic that followed us around the rest of the day, our duckies followed us everywhere. We dressed them in diapers, tied ribbons gently around their necks for leashes and took them out for a walk around the block.

We couldn't take the duckies to bed with us. They shivered in their cardboard box under the kitchen table. One by one, loved-to-death, the squeaking fluffy ducklings fell and didn't get up.

Because we didn't know what else to do, Dad found a shiny cigar box in his workbench room, and helped us line it with fake grass from our Easter baskets. We placed our quiet ducklings in the white and gold cigar box and quietly closed the lid.

We carried it to the back yard and buried it. My sister and I cried and sang prayers from church. My brother played in the sandbox.

The Truth About Christmas

Every November, when I turn the calendar to Thanksgiving, I think about the real beginning of the holiday season. As much as I look forward to the family reunions, I begin to get that sinking feeling...in my day planner.

Many of my friends echo the same refrain. They complain, *We do the shopping. We do the baking. We do the cooking and the decorating.*

We definitely do the wrapping.

Ok, so things are changing, I argue. Men seem to be helping more around the house these days, lending a hand with the housework and decorations. I've heard that some men will even iron, and that's good, because around the holidays, everybody has something that needs ironing. A few good men will notice the stress level rising, before it starts simmering like hot cider.

My favorite story about holiday burnout comes from my friend Gloria, who raised six boys on a farm, back in the days before dishwashers.

The story goes that every Christmas morning, after weeks of preparations plus all the usual daily labor known to farmers, Gloria would get up at the crack of dawn with her boys, watch them tear open their boxes, with wrapping paper flying everywhere, and wait to see their smiles of delight.

Then, she would go to her bedroom, close the door and cry. In about a half hour, she'd dry her face, go back downstairs and start cooking Christmas dinner. Her husband, Jim, who did not necessarily lack compassion, would just shake his head and say, "Not again this year..."

Well, one year, my friend slipped on the ice and broke both arms.

Guess who had to do all the shopping, the wrapping, and the...well, you know. On that particular Christmas morning, after watching the boys unwrap their gifts, Gloria and Jim both went off to separate corners of the estate to vent.

He went out to the barn to kick around a wooden bucket. He couldn't believe what a job it was just to get all the sizes and colors right for the boys. She went up to her bedroom, exhausted by what she could do and overwhelmed by what she couldn't. She had a good Christmas cry, but when she dried her face, she saw an angel of irony smiling at her, and Gloria started laughing out loud.

She knew that she would never again race around with a frantic pulse and a list that only ended on Christmas morning. Gloria promised the angel that before she felt like decking the clerk at the all-night supermarket, she would go home and take the evening for herself.

Gloria shares this story, because even though she is a grandmother today, she remembers vividly the feeling of the Christmas candle burning at both ends. She says she thought she was the only one to feel that way during the holidays.

Gloria has a glass angel in an old wooden bucket next to her fireplace. It stays out all year.

Amaryllis

Dear Amaryllis,

You haven't answered my letters.

Our hurricane of misunderstandings and accusations has passed, but the wreckage, like an empty wooden rowboat wedged into the sand, remains strewn across the beach.

I think the storm between us began in the clouds of losses in both our lives: my husband's father, his mother, his sister-in-law. I lost my job. I had a hysterectomy. You lost your grandmother, the final link in the invisible chain of your grandfather, father, and mother.

Since this death between us, I've wept almost daily, rubbing a cramp of bitter emptiness in my chest.

I've spit cherry pits of profanity into the air, as if you could see me, as if you chewed the fruit the same as I.

I send this letter to you.

I call you Amaryllis, because like you, the flower grows naturally long, graceful and feminine. The perennial thrives in hot lush climate and the flower blooms as stunning as red chile pepper, makes everyone stop and catch their breath and smile.

I think of myself as gardenia, fragrant but monochrome, moonlight to your sun. But Amaryllis, you are right out there, radiant fire engine red.

From the very first time we met, I loved you. I felt right away that we would be friends, like we had known each other forever, perhaps because we had so much in common. You were an aspiring singer and entertainer, and I was an aspiring writer and musician.

I recognized at once, and I think you did too, a creative bridge, a song between us.

Perhaps because we are each excellent cooks. Your cauliflower and cheese pie, my chicken stew. Your pesto, my stuffed grape leaves. Nobody beats your cheesecake. Don't you miss my gazpacho?

We came together in the first place because of my husband. You've been his friend for twenty-five years. I've been his wife for ten.

Together, we've howled his sense of humor, applauded his knack for fiscal geometry and known his kindness. We both share his love.

Amaryllis, we both came from childhoods of chaos. Our fathers were alcoholic and eventually abandoned us. Our mothers, raised devout Catholic and obedient, both went to the priest for help with the urgent utility bills and the kids with no underwear. In the darkness of the confessional, they were told, *Pray, obey your husbands and keep your families together.*

Advice which was answered with compliance, the kind of compliance that kills, if you ask me. You know, I never met your mother, the breast cancer finished her just days before we met. Did you know that my mother was hospitalized several times for *nervous breakdown*, a condition which means to the child inside of me, a woman crying uncontrollably, sobbing hysterically for hours, and being taken away.

To this day, I can't forgive the church for that—although you are strongly religious and I respect your choice. I thank God for the bouquet of love in my life today, and for meeting you.

Remember when we realized that insanity can be clarity, a step toward survival and a whole life?

During our hurricane, while you were screaming and swirling, you called me cold and controlling. You thought I was making plans behind your back and trying to exclude you. You were wrong.

I was reeling in the eye of the wreckage. I was over-protecting you. I failed to treat you as a responsible grown-up. I was wrong.

But my God, what could have happened to cause you to drop my flowerpot, my bulbs in clay?

Nothing you could have said or done would have caused me to throw you out like garbage, short of sleeping with my husband or eating one of my children.

Even then, I would have called you back in three or four days, wondering what we could do to sort this out. Yet, you did the next worst thing—you took away my best friend.

For that, I could eat your eyes like pearl onions and salt your lilac bushes.

Instead, I've missed you. I've missed your voice, clear Joan Baez soprano, and your laugh, pure Betty Grable. I've missed your daughter starting kindergarten and your baby turning two.

You've missed my daughter starting first grade and reading out loud on her first day of school. She's read a hundred books since then. She has a list.

Don't you miss me? Won't you forgive me?

Isn't the hurricane just one mark in time, one minute in the lifetime of our friendship, one color in the garden? Our history seeds and reseeds, like a field of milkweed. We breastfed our babies together.

We shared family vacations on your beach at Lake Michigan, and while our children played in the sand with their Daddies, we dared each other into the clear cold water, running with waves to waist deep and chasing the water just over our heads.

When I jumped into the water, I waited to hear you scream with exhilaration. You scream tribal.

What did *you* wait for?

Amaryllis, we put our art on hold for awhile, so we could feast in the joy of being with our children. We were sometimes the only ones who understood the rub when asked, *You're not working? How do you stand being home all day?* which meant, *You must be stupid.*

I know that you are going to have all the dreams of your life come true. You'll be a singer, a teacher, or something else you haven't thought of yet.

I am just beginning to harvest the seedlings in my greenhouse. I have a wonderful family, like you—a man who works as hard as I do, deserves my praise, and tends his garden. When he brushes his cheek on my petals, I know they have never been so fragrant, or the foliage so green. I am practicing my art again, and I am writing. *I'm writing to you.*

In the Raw

Nancy Ryan

Writing is a matter of survival for me, a way of simultaneously making sense of and shaping my world. When I write, the things that keep me up at night creep onto paper. Sometimes they surprise me, peeking out of a sentence or paragraph and then demanding more space. Sometimes they surprise others. My writing style was once described as a narrative form of *cinéma vérité*, another term for candid camera, the recording of life and people as they are, *in the raw,* a description I find intriguing. My love of cinema and drama has undoubtedly influenced my writing, encouraging me to try to capture my characters and settings versus create them. I am also influenced by the voice of my grandfather, who could really tell a story.

Skating on Spice

I held the snow globe in both hands and shook it, bringing it up to eye level as the confetti-like flakes fell. My mind drifted like snow blown by a western wind. Across the years, red- and blue-scarved skaters did figure eights and serpentines on opaque white ice. One of the skaters, a girl of fifteen with chin-length brown ringlets and mink-like eyes, scanned Lake St. Clair for "spice," sea-green ice as smooth and translucent as aspic. Further out, the girl could almost see such ice.

The snow slowly coated the pink-cheeked skaters and dulled the blades of their skates. The girl dug the tip of her left skate into the crusty ice and pushed off with her right. She worked her way toward the glistening ice, but it seemed much further away than she had thought. Yet she finally did reach it, pirouetting when she found that the spice was just as splendid as she had imagined.

Near the middle of the lake, the snow fell faster but softer, dissolving like sugar upon the spice. The girl bent over, smiling as a series of bubbles floated upward at the same speed as the falling snow. She thought she saw a fish inch by—a bass or a perch, perhaps—and wondered how many others were moving like a whisper beneath her. Then she straightened, spinning around and skating off backwards, hips swinging like a figure skater's.

The spice creaked. The girl pivoted toward the shore, sure that another skater had followed. But she saw no one through the steady blanket of snow. She turned again and glided forward. The spice creaked louder. The girl spun into a stop and glanced over her shoulder, again seeing nothing. She looked back down, and this time she saw skate marks on the spice. She followed the trail made by the skates, first to the east and then to the west, a bit to the north. . .

She looked toward the shore again, but the snow was falling harder now, and she could see no skaters. They had gone on without her, or had she gone on without them? It made no difference, really. She was skating on thin ice, alone but not alone, in the middle of the spice, in the middle of the lake, in the middle of the winter, late in the day.

The skate marks were gone, too, swept under a flying white carpet.

The girl made fists in her mittens and started toward the shore, which was sandwiched between dusk and driving snow. Skating fast, she tried to ignore the pains shooting through her feet, which begged for release from her skates. When the ice to her fore crackled loudly, as if struck by lightening from below, the girl skidded to a halt, afraid to move forward, afraid to move back.

Dusk had melted into dark, and she could see a dim half-moon quietly chiding her. She took a half-dozen steps forward, then dropped onto the ice. Her calves trembled and her thighs stung, and she wasn't even sure if she was still facing the shore. She reached out a hand and captured a handful of lacy flakes, cupping them in the dark of her palm. But when she opened her palm they, too, were gone, like the skate marks, and the spice, and the light.

She crossed herself and began saying the Lord's Prayer. A voice floated down from the moon.

Ghost Lake's a dark lake, a deep lake and cold.
Ice black as ebony, frostily scrolled.

The voice floated up from the lake itself.

Far in its shadows a faint sound whirrs;
Steep stand the sentineled deep dark firs.

The words, from "The Skater of Ghost Lake," one of her favorite poems, were William Rose Benet's; the voice, her father's.

Through the embossings of snow, the girl could see that the ice had darkened. When the voice reached the last stanza, a pale figure moved to her side. Jack Frost, she thought deliriously, for the figure was clothed in white and covered with snow, or Jesus Christ, come to take her home. The figure raised one arm, gesturing upward and then to the right. "Rise up," it said. "Go forth." The girl rose, numbly following the white shroud, which glowed like a candle against the dark ice. When she stumbled, it beckoned; when she stopped, it paused. When she toppled onto the shore, it disappeared.

"Skating on Spice" is an excerpt from a novel-in-progress entitled *Ghost Walkers*.

Bat Girl

It was the second night she'd spent in jail. It was before commencement. It was before prom. It was two days after her eighteenth birthday. She was wearing flannel underwear with red hearts on them under gray sweats, wool socks under fleece-lined moccasins. She'd just finished the pasty her mom had brought her. She was huddled in the northwest corner of the cell, trying to stay clear of the bird that was doing hang-gliding maneuvers in front of her. It flew by her. It was as scared as she was. But it wasn't a bird. It was a bat.

*

Jeannie crawled around the cell, trying to second guess where the bat would go next. The cell, a 12' x 12' corner of Timber Lake's 36' x 36' jail, had two outside walls and two connecting sets of bars. Jeannie wondered briefly why the bat didn't just fly through the bars.

"Don't worry," the lady deputy said, sliding the cell door open and grabbing the blanket off Jeannie's bed. "They don't really get in your hair."

The bat landed on a bar six feet down. The lady deputy inched toward it with the blanket held high, as if catching bats was an everyday thing for her. Jeannie winced, anticipating the catch.

Afterward, she laid on the steel-frame bed and tried to remember just how it happened. It was like a magic act. The bat was there one minute, under the blanket the next. It was like the night of her party. Jimmy was walking alongside the road one minute, under the tires of her mom's Chevette the next. She fell asleep wondering about Jimmy, and bats, and whether anyone would believe her if she told them that a bat flew across her windshield and caused the Chevette to swerve.

That night, Jeannie dreamt she was moving through a dark cave lined with curtains of fur. She stumbled into a furry chamber filled with whispers. As her eyes adjusted to the light, the curtains folded inward and the whispers came louder and faster. A dozen bats swooped down before her and began climbing up her pants legs, making chattering sounds.

"Help! Somebody help!" Wide awake, Jeannie could still hear herself screaming the words.

When Sheriff Jarvie arrived at ten, he let her call her mom. Jeannie wondered why he was being so nice. Maybe to buck the lady deputy, who usually worked the county jail. Maybe because he'd grown up with her dad, who'd up and left three years ago for the Florida Gulf. He had a trailer there, white with blue shutters and only two miles from the ocean. Jeannie had a picture of it taped to her bedroom dresser.

She'd stayed there with Jimmy and Shirley Ray for a whole week last summer. They'd had a morning ritual: smoke two joints after Jeannie's dad left and then set off for the Gulf on foot, crossing the bridge at Madeira Beach by noon. By Friday, Jeannie'd turned salmon pink, but Jimmy and Shirley Ray'd gotten cocoa brown and started calling each other "twin." Jimmy'd rubbed Coppertone on Shirley Ray's back and they'd taken off together for the little stores at John's Pass, coming back with homemade waffle cones and braided friendship bracelets. As they played in the surf, Jeannie'd buried her feet in the sand and watched rainbow-colored speedboats sink into the horizon. "Go drown yourself," she'd told Jimmy when he grabbed her crotch that night at the trailer. And when Shirley Ray said she was sorry the next morning, Jeannie'd barked "woof woof" and thrown a chameleon in her face.

"Jeannie," her mom said, breaking the thought. "Got these from the corner store." She perched on the chair outside the cell and pulled a bouquet of plastic daisies, a pack of Rockin' Raspberry bubble gum, and a red ski hat and mittens out of a dirty canvas bag.

"They're pretty." Jeannie tossed the daisies on the bed and put on the hat and mittens. "Thanks for bringing my stuff. Where's the paper?"

"Your father called last night. He can't come."

Jeannie swallowed. "But he'll send money?"

"Money's tight right now. You got much money saved for Florida?"

"My Florida money?" Jeannie tore into the bubble gum, casting a sideways look at her mom. "I don't know. . .couple of hundred."

"These things cost," Jeannie's mom said, glancing around the cell. "I got a lawyer—Norm Bates. Nice young man from the city. Sheriff Jarvie knows him."

Jeannie jammed a piece of bubble gum into her mouth. "I don't want no lawyer named Norman Bates. It'll remind everybody of *Psycho*."

"Not Norman. Norm. You just tell him what happened. And stay out of trouble."

"I already got in that."

"Sheriff said you had a rough night."

"It's cold in here. And there's bats."

"Bats? They get in your hair." Her mom smoothed her own mouse-brown hair. "Oh, Lord. Can't believe they're making such a big deal about a few beers. If Jimmy and Shirley Ray hadn't taken off like that. . ."

When her mom rose to leave a few minutes later, Jeannie reached between the bars for the canvas bag. "Where's the paper?"

"Forgot it at home," her mom said, pulling the bag away.

"Anything in it on me?"

"Nothing to write home about. You worry about what you're gonna tell Norm Bates, not what people say. He's due any minute now."

"You got a paper?" Jeannie asked Sheriff Jarvie an hour later. She'd made the front page again. It was all there. The party. The fight. The warrant and arraignment. "If Jim Halonen dies," she read, chewing harder on her gum, "Jeannie Kukkola may be charged with driving under the influence and voluntary manslaughter." She spit the gum out when her left eye, as shiny as a frozen blueberry, started to throb.

"Saw Doc Wallis last night at the carnival," Sheriff Jarvie said, shaking his head. "Jimmy's still in a coma. Did that lady deputy really catch that bat?"

"Yep." Jeannie pulled the ski hat over her ears and read on. There were pictures of her and Jimmy, pictures taken for the *Timber Lake High School Yearbook* last fall.

"How long it take her?"

"Ten minutes." Manslaughter. She'd seen the word before, but it looked funny. Man's laughter. *Man's laughter.* She wondered why Norm Bates was late.

"How'd she do it?" the sheriff asked.

"With a blanket."

"Did she kill it or loose it?"

Jeannie shrugged. "I don't know. She just took it away. Is Norm Bates real good?"

"*Real* good. Got my nephew Will off the hook. You remember Will—had a few too many after the fishfly festival and drove his Jeep through

Jappinens' living room window."

Jeannie crossed her fingers: Please don't let Norm Bates look like Norman Bates. She uncrossed her fingers when Sheriff Jarvie lead him in a couple minutes later. He had short brown hair and was on the skinny side, but he looked more like Ferris Bueller than Norman Bates. No nervous tic. No stutter.

Norm Bates tapped his foot while Jeannie talked. She noticed his shoes, shiny black loafers with little tassels on them, his matching black briefcase, his navy pinstripe suit and black wool topcoat. She wondered how he got to be a lawyer. If he grew up in a place like Timber Lake but somehow made it out. If he'd ever been in jail. He doesn't like me, she decided, trying to see what he was writing on his yellow legal pad. He thinks I deserve this. That I'm lowlife.

"Let's go over it again," Norm Bates said, eyes skimming the legal pad. "You were going around the bend, speed about forty, and saw someone walking on the side of the road. Then you hit a patch of ice and lost control of the car."

"And I hit something." Jeannie looked down at her hands. A piece of red yarn was dangling from the wrist of her left mitten. She slipped off her right mitten and pulled on it. "Jimmy. Jimmy was walking on the side of the road." The piece of yarn kept getting longer, like the trail of blood across Old 21. She looked up. "I'd had a couple beers."

"At your birthday party. How many beers?"

"I don't know. Just a few beers. Jimmy had some, too. He left with Shirley Ray, my best friend."

"It says here that you'd had a fight and were both legally drunk."

She looked back down. The mitten was unravelling in her hands.

Norm Bates cleared his throat. "Anything else you'd like to tell me?"

Jeannie touched her blackened left eye. "Jimmy was drunker."

"Will Shirley Ray vouch for that?"

"I don't know. Probably can't remember."

Norm Bates stared at her, as if he wanted to dig deeper. "Do you have any questions?" he asked finally, putting the legal pad into the black briefcase.

"The trial. When will it be?"

Norm Bates shrugged.

Jeannie wound the yarn around her index finger. Everyone in Timber

Lake would probably show. Not much else to do in late April except go to Chubbie's, the corner bar her next-door neighbor owned. The leftover snow was yellow, the ground soft as horse manure, the lake a bowl of slush.

"How long will it last?"

"That depends," Norm Bates said, putting on his coat and backing away from her. "How do you want to plead?"

"Plead?"

"You know. Guilty, not guilty. . ."

"Mind if I think about it?"

She couldn't stop thinking about it. The paper said Jimmy might die. When she closed her eyes, Jeannie could almost see him standing alongside the road, smiling crookedly and giving her the bird. She leaned over the Chevette's console and rolled down the passenger window, flinging her ring at him. Then the car swerved. Or Jimmy ran in front of it. She wasn't sure which—or even if it mattered. It was a big mess, like one of those mind-boggling algebra problems with lots of different equations but only one solution. If only there had been a bat.

A hour later, Sheriff Jarvie went home for lunch, returning with a pankulla square and a torn copy of *Modern Maturity.*

"Article in here about bats," he said. "Thought you might like to read it."

"Going batty," the headline read. "Rescuing the reputation of America's most maligned mammal." Jeannie skimmed the article while picking at the pankulla. Bats are misunderstood. Bats don't get in your hair. Bats are not flying mice. Bats seldom carry rabies. Few wild creatures have suffered greater persecution than bats.

✷

Jeannie lay down on the bed and thought about Jimmy and the trial. She picked up the daisies her mom brought and laid them on her chest, imagining herself walking through a white and yellow field warmed by a midday sun. She remembered picking daisies with Shirley Ray two summers ago and then sitting on the back porch and pulling off the petals, one by one, and daydreaming about Jimmy: "He loves me, he loves me not. He loves me, he loves me not. He loves me!"

"They loose me," she said aloud, pulling off one, then another, of the shiny plastic petals. "They loose me not."

She started to pluck the remaining petals but then stopped. She'd seen it in Norm Bates' eyes: Guilty until proven innocent, and proof was as slippery as Old 21 after seven beers. She shivered, wrapping the dark gray blanket around her body and dropping her head to her knees.

"They loose me and they loose me not."

"Jeannie?" a man's voice said a long time later.

Jeannie looked up to find Norm Bates staring down at her.

"Jeannie, they've reduced the charges. You'll have to appear for driving under the influence, but you're free to go. Your mom's on her way."

"Free?"

Norm Bates gave Jeannie a long look before leaving. She waited for him to say something, like "Stay out of trouble" or "Anything else you'd like to tell me?" But he just stared, sober brown eyes assuring her that nothing had really changed.

"Can't say I'll miss this place," Jeannie told Sheriff Jarvie as he led her from her cell. But when the sun touched her face she shivered, wishing she was in Siberia or the Bermuda Triangle or a dark cave lined with fur.

Finger Exercises

On the third bar of *The Smoker's Reflection*, Anita caught fire. Upon finishing the song, she lifted up her hands and splayed her fingers. "Not bad for an old girl," she said, flicking a lock of bottled blonde hair out of her eyes. She flipped to page twelve of *Bach for Beginners* and played *Minuet in* G *Major*, mottled fingers caressing the keys. She took a swig of Irish Mist and lit a cigarette when finished, inhaling deeply and wondering: Is piano better the second time around?

Anita patted the seat of the old Woodward, which she'd bought some forty years before from the blind pianist who'd ignited the ivories at the Ritz Carlton. A month after that she was still trying to play her favorite song, with her best friend, Lillian, singing along: "Jeepers Creepers! Where'd ya get those peepers? Jeepers Creepers! Where'd ya get those eyes?" Soon after that she met Ben, who looked like Ronald Reagan and said she had Jeepers-Creepers eyes. And soon after that she'd retired the piano. Until six months ago when they retired, and Anita had time on her hands. She thought they would travel after selling their insurance business—or at least do things together. But Ben traded being tied to the office to being tied to the TV.

"You won't believe what just happened on *General Hospital*," Ben said, strolling into the room and placing a sweating bottle of Stroh's atop the piano. "Robert Scorpio's dead wife—you know, Holly—isn't really dead."

"What did you expect?" Anita asked, reaching for the decanter of Irish Mist on top of the piano and pouring herself three fingers. "How's Audrey?"

"Not on enough."

Good, Anita thought. The other day Ben said that looking at Audrey Hardy got him hard, and Anita instantly hated her. She was so slim. So stylish. So intact. She wished that Audrey Hardy would have a hysterectomy, too. Then, six months or so later, Dr. Hardy could take her to bed, showing Ben and GH fans at large that women without uteruses can make love, too.

"Watch the piano," she said instead, grinding out her cigarette and swooping up Ben's beer. "I just had it refinished and tuned."

"Could you have the stove tuned, too? I'm starved."

Anita peered at her watch. "Four o'clock," she said, handing Ben his beer and lowering her hands to the keyboard. "I've got another hour of practice. Then I'll fix something."

"Forget it. I'll fix something myself."

"There's Kentucky Fried Chicken in the freezer. Breasts. You still like breasts, don't you?"

"Yep," Ben said. "But I think I'll watch Oprah first. God, it's smoky in here, Nita. Lay off the smokes, won't you?"

"Where there's smoke, there's fire." The old adage had once applied, Anita thought, remembering their twentieth anniversary, when Ben reserved a suite at the Ritz Carlton and lined it with four dozen red carnations, six bottles of Moet & Chandon champagne, and three dozen escargo. They drank the champagne and ate the escargo, got in a rip-roaring fight, flung the carnations at each other, and finished off one hell of a night by making love in the sunken bathtub.

"Where there's fire, there's a fire extinguisher," Anita said as Ben walked away, sure that he'd put a damper on any romantic getaway she might plan nowadays.

✷

"Ben," Anita called out an hour later. "Ben, you've got to hear this."

"Hear what?" he asked from the doorway.

"This." Anita flipped over a tattered piece of sheet music and began pounding on the keyboard.

"*Jeepers Creepers*. What's so new about that?"

"For the first time in my life," she said, turning toward him, "the first, thank you!—I played the bass. The bass!"

"It was wonderful."

"You're not at all interested, are you? Don't you see what this means?"

"Yes, I do see. You've been playing only half of *Jeepers Creepers* your whole life, and now you can play the whole thing. I'm happy for you. For us."

Anita turned back toward the piano. "There you go again."

"That's Ronald Reagan's line. Come on, Nita, let's eat."

In the midst of her third chicken leg, Anita began laughing hysterically. "If only you'd seen your face."

Ben scowled. "I see my face every day. And every day it looks older."

Anita turned her head sideways and lowered her voice. "'You've been playing only half of *Jeepers Creepers* your whole life, and now you can play the whole thing,'" she mimicked. "'I'm happy for you. For us.' Ha!"

"I am. Really. Now you can move on to something new."

"A new song? I already know three new songs. *The Smoker's Reflection*, *Minuet in G Major*, and *The Desert Song*."

Ben stopped eating, holding his chicken wing in mid-air. "You can play *The Desert Song*? I love that song."

"I know." Anita wiped her fingers with her napkin and motioned for Ben to follow her to the piano. She concentrated on each note, hitting the keys with studied precision, then glanced over at Ben, who was slumped in the brown vinyl recliner across from her, eyes closed.

"Beautiful," he said, humming along.

Anita's fingers began humming, too, as if they didn't even need the piano. But when she reached the final refrain, the notes on the sheet music blurred and a cold numbness crept up her fingertips to her hands to her arms. "Call 911," she whispered, slumping forward on the piano.

✷

Dr. Hinshaw shrugged. "We'll know more after we do a few more tests. But you're doing fine now. Just fine."

"What happened?"

"Probably a small stroke. Doesn't appear to be any permanent damage. But you need to watch your blood pressure. And make those changes we discussed."

"I know, I know. Quit smoking and start eating right. And try to relax."

Anita sunk down in the hospital bed, wondering how many cigarettes she'd smoked in the last fifty years, how many fried chicken legs she'd eaten, how many bottles of Stroh's and glasses of Irish Mist she'd drank. Dr. Hinshaw hadn't mentioned the booze, but it couldn't have helped. She'd drank even more since retiring. Something to do.

She flicked on the TV and flipped through the channels, stopping when she reached Channel 7. *General Hospital.* She peered at the small TV screen to the left of the hospital bed, wondering which of the young beauties was Holly, the dead wife who'd never been dead. She'd watched the soap some ten summers ago, during a slow period at the office. But other than Audrey none of the characters looked familiar—except that red-haired nurse who'd faked blindness in order to wrap some hot-shot doctor around her finger. A clever deception, Anita thought, looking down at her hands.

When Ben walked into Anita's room a half hour later, she was sitting up and trying to flex her right hand. "Just saw Dr. Hinshaw," Ben said, pulling a gold vinyl chair up to the hospital bed and plopping into it. "He said not to worry, that it was just a little stroke."

"I know," Anita said, sniffling and wiping her eyes with the corner of the sheet.

"Then why are you crying?"

"I'm not crying," she sniffled, looking up at Ben. "It's just that. . ."

"Just what?"

"No. You'll think it's silly."

"Try me."

Anita made a sound somewhere between a giggle and a sob. "It's just that it took me fifty years to learn how to play the bass. And now I won't even be able to play the melody. My right hand's still numb."

"For God's sake, Nita. Instead of being glad you're alive you're worrying about that damned piano. Besides, Dr. Hinshaw says you're doing fine. . ."

"I am. I am. Except for my right hand. It's numb, Ben."

✷

"Can I get you something?" Ben asked, awkwardly fluffing a pillow and placing it behind Anita's head.

"I can do for myself," Anita said, adjusting the pillow and reaching for the brown and gold afghan on the back of Ben's recliner.

"Come on, Anita. Just for once, let me help."

Anita let Ben tuck the afghan around her body. "Thanks."

"You had me worried, Nita. Dr. Hinshaw said to take it easy—just do things you enjoy for awhile." Ben paused. "Sorry I said that about your piano. I'm probably just jealous—never had the touch with things like that."

The next day, Anita sat at the piano but didn't lay a finger on it. The day after that, she played scales on it with her left hand. And the day after that, she wrote a "for sale" advertisement and called it in to *The Thurston Crier.*

"Sorry, but the piano's been sold," she told a man who called the day after the advertisement ran. "Let me take your number, just in case they don't pick it up."

"Pick what up?" Ben asked, rounding the corner from the kitchen with a plate of green-apple slices and bagels.

"The piano," Anita said, glaring at him. "I'm selling the piano, that's all."

"Come on, Nita. It'll all come back to you. I can't believe it . . . I honestly miss your songs. Even *Jeepers Creepers.*"

Ben had that pug-dog look on his face that always softened Anita up, and she was almost sorry about lying to him.

"Nita, I've got an idea," he said after they finished lunch.

Anita shrugged, leaning back in the recliner. "What kind of an idea?"

"You could teach me how to play the piano. It would stay fresh in your mind that way. And we could work your hand at the same time."

Anita snorted. "Teach you?"

"Yeah. Why not?"

"It would never work. To begin with, I can barely talk without using my hands. And you can't even read music."

"That's the beauty of it," Ben said, rising. "I'll be your hands. Come on."

Anita raised her eyebrows as Ben walked to the piano and sat down, but she didn't budge.

"Come on," he said again.

"I can't," she said, trying to clench her right hand.

Ben ran his fingers from the top to the bottom of the keyboard. "I'm not getting up until I can play the first ten notes of *The Desert Song.*"

"You'll die of thirst first."

"Fine," Ben said, playing chopsticks over and over again. "If you won't teach me *The Desert Song*, I'll play the only song I know."

Anita giggled as Ben thumped on the piano like a child. "Okay!" she said finally. "Move to the right."

Ben scooted over, and Anita sat down on his left.

"This is C," she told him, pointing to a key in the middle of the keyboard with her left index finger. "This is where it all starts." Anita did an octave with her left hand. "C, D, E, F, G, A, B, C. . . See?"

Ben nodded.

"Lucky for you, *The Desert Song* begins with C. It's easy to remember." Anita played the first six notes with her left hand. "C, B, G, B, C, G," she recited aloud.

"Okay, okay. Let me try."

Anita giggled again as Ben tried to mimic her actions. "You may as well use your right hand. Come on, try it again."

"God, this is hard," Ben said, switching hands.

"And then there's the bass. . ."

"No way, Anita. That's where you come in."

"Me?"

"Yep. Until you can do the right hand again—the melody, is that what you call it?—you can play the bass."

"We're going to play together?"

"Yep," Ben said, placing her right hand under his on the keyboard and rhythmically massaging her fingers.

Roberta's Lover

That moment she was mine, mine, fair,
Perfectly pure and good: I found
A thing to do, and all her hair
In one long yellow string I wound
Three times her little throat around,
And strangled her. No pain felt she;
I am quite sure she felt no pain.

From "Porphyria's Lover," Robert Browning

Berta peers at me from polished black marble, a woman carved in stone.

I lean closer, trying to read her chiseled lips. I trace her eyebrows, her nose, the two-foot braid looped at the base of her neck like a noose. I promised Berta that I'd never leave her alone, so I come whenever I can, come and think about how Berta ended up here, stuck between "Our Little Angel" and "Mary Magadalene" in Lantern Lake Cemetery.

I lean to the left and imagine walking down the aisle of the Lantern Lake Presbyterian Church with Berta. People are throwing rice, and it sticks in my hair like bird shit, and isn't that just the way Berta ended up treating me anyway? When I move back to center, I'm on top of Berta again, and I can almost see why people called us brother and sister: dark brown hair and eyes, patrician nose, licorice-thin lips.

Then Berta's stony face begins to move. "I'm sorry I. . ." she starts to say, but I lean to the right before she can finish.

When we were in Mrs. Boyle's twelfth grade creative writing class at Lantern Lake High, I'd write Berta notes on pale blue line paper, and she'd scribble on the bottom of them and slip them back. I wrote Berta poems, too, poems about seeing in the dark and love at first sight, but I never read them aloud or gave them to her. And she wrote poems of her own, but they weren't anything like mine. Berta wrote about saving the whales, soldiers who died in Desert Storm, bag ladies who slept in cardboard boxes in Detroit. I'd pretend that she was Elizabeth Barrett and I was Robert Browning, but then creative writing class ended, and

Berta took up tennis.

Beneath Berta's face, two tennis rackets face off, tennis ball suspended between them. I close my eyes and reach for it.

✷

Berta backed away from the net, moving back, way back, left foot inches from the base line. She lobbed the ball toward me, and I lobbed it back. Back, forth, forth, back, I blew her kisses between shots while A.J. Smith looked on.

"Fifteen—love," Berta said, flicking her braid over her left shoulder and smoothing her yellow tennis skirt with both hands. She fired a cannonball at me—and then another and another—as A.J. Smith moved in.

"Easy, Berta," I said, but the shots came harder and faster, till I could hear my heart in my head and feel my face burn hot-pepper red.

"Forty—love." Berta flashed A.J. Smith her Madonna smile and slammed the ball past me.

"Out!" I yelled, but she was already driving another one my way.

✷

When I open my eyes, I can still see her, racket-shaped nebula grasped in her right hand, shooting stars at me from heaven.

The Lantern Lake P.D. called it a "crime of passion" and threw A.J. in the slammer. He had the murder weapon all right, iron-fist hands with Berta's name tattooed on them. And then there was "A Riddle for Roberta," neatly typed on the back side of a grocery bag:

Mystery and intrigue is the game.
The prize is diamonds for the dame,
but you must show to stake your claim.
I give you two clues without shame:
the first is that I have some fame,
the second, that you share my name.

A.J. Smith has fame all right, more fame than he'll ever know what to do with, thanks to Berta and me. And to think that he was once a measly packing boy at the IGA who fought lightweights in his spare time.

I look up, feeling the sun warm my neck like Berta's breath used to do.

*

"Like it?" she asked, twirling on one leg in a strapless pink-flamingo dress, half-drunk on love and pink champagne.

"Take it off," I said as she spun around again. "The ring. Take it off."

Berta looked at me and then at the gold band glinting on her ring finger. "No way." She made a fist, curled fingers choosing A.J. Smith over me. "We got it in Vegas. I'll get a diamond when A.J. wins a fight." She leaned against the wrought-iron fence that separated the park by Lantern Lake from the cemetery and folded her arms across her breasts. A blue heron dove through the trees and landed some twenty feet from us, and the cicadas hummed overhead, but aside from that, we were alone.

"Give it to me!" I pushed Berta up against the fence, pried her arms apart, and tried to wrench the ring off her finger.

"Leave me alone," she cried as the pink dress slipped beneath her pink breasts.

"Never." Berta sidestepped away from me, left hand behind her back. I grabbed her right arm and pulled her to the ground. "And that's a promise."

*

I pinch my nostrils, trying to ignore the dead-fish odor that drifts up from Lantern Lake on balmy August days. But the odor won't go away. It's coming from Berta, my Berta, who thought she was so smart, running off to Vegas with A.J. Smith and getting hitched like that.

And then Berta isn't carved in stone anymore. She's sitting on the ground beside me, staring at her reflection in polished black granite and fiddling with her braid.

"I'm sorry I wouldn't take off my ring," she says.

"I'll forgive you this time," I say, fingering her braid. "Just don't do it again."

"And I'm sorry I ran off with A.J. Smith instead of you."

"I'm sorry, too, Berta," I say, unclasping the gold barrette that joins the braid's head and tail. "Just don't do it again."

"And I'm sorry I slammed the ball at you like that. I'll never do it again."

"I know you won't, Berta," I say, wrapping the braid around her neck and pulling it taut, pulling it till Berta says no more.

I remember removing the ring from her finger and throwing it in Lantern Lake.

I remember dragging Berta in after it.

I remember standing there in the water, holding onto her braid. It looked like some kind of road kill, all matted and wet and limp, so I cut it off with my Bowie knife, put it in a brown paper bag, and buried it in the sales office parking lot, under the sign that says "CE-ME-TRY."

And then Berta's a woman carved in stone again, and I can't read her lips or see beyond her eyes. So I sit at her feet and read her my favorite poem, "Porphyria's Lover" by Robert Browning. She knows it by heart now, just like I do.

In the Raw

We walk hand in hand through the sun-pierced darkness of the Taquamenon Falls State Park, past a sinewy beech with a vine-like trunk and a wilted wild orchid without any leaves. The beech and the orchid make me want to cry. Sometimes I still feel like that orchid, stripped naked but trying to last just one more day. And the beech is almost as twisted as Don, the guy who's married to Aunt Pauline.

I stop when Jake stops. He's not so wired now, and his eyes have that new-baby look they had when I first met him. But then he started working double shifts at Huffy's, even though there's a recession going on, because people would rather dump their nickels and dimes into old boats than spend their dollars on new lemons, and his eyes started looking like blue poker chips. Jake's '78 brown Catalina is a boat, but chances are he'll get us to Aunt Pauline's this afternoon—even if I put sugar in the gas tank or a banana in the tailpipe or something like that. Jake's one great mechanic, even if he didn't finish high school and smokes too much CAT.

Jake grew up in the city; he's never been north of the Mackinac Bridge before. I took three days off from the Silver Stirrups—the strip joint where I dance—to come north with him. Not just to Mackinaw City, and Taquamenon, but to Whitefish Point. Jake's always wanted to see Whitefish Point, which is just north of Shelldrake Lake, where my Aunt Pauline lives. And now he wants to meet Aunt Pauline, too.

Fifteen years later and 70 pounds heavier, I tell myself it's going to be different this time, but the truth is, I don't really want to go to Aunt Pauline's at all. It's not your usual set of reasons—not "I spent every summer there as a kid," not "It's just a dot on the map," not "We've kind of lost touch." It's Don. He likes little girls. At least he did when I knew him. Skinny little girls with red, French-braided hair who wore Carter's underwear and had no mom except Aunt Pauline. Skinny little girls he'd play strip poker with. And other games like that.

The problem is, I've got to go. There's $2,000 riding on it, $2,000 to buy some nice clothes from Hudson's and get me and Jake off to a good start. Not to mention piece of mind. It's like Oprah said—you've got to confront your perpetrator. You've got to make him pay.

I follow Jake toward a sunbeam on the edge of the forest, toward the fizzling waterfall called Taquamenon. We lean our heads back and watch the frothy water shoot over the rocks, like a jet of root beer.

"Taquamenon," Jake says slowly, but it sounds like "Take-on-a-man."

"Ta-qua-me-naw," I whisper.

I couldn't say it right, either, till we read "The Song of Hiawatha" in seventh grade. In the forest by the "Taquamenaw"—that's where Hiawatha lived. Hiawatha was something, uniting the Iroquois against the Alongonquin like that and using magic to protect them from evil. That summer, when Grandma sent me back to Aunt Pauline's, I prayed to Hiawatha, prayed that he'd protect me, and all other girls like me, from Don. But I wasn't an Iroquois, and Hiawatha didn't hear my prayer.

✷

When we pull onto north 23, which will take us straight through Paradise to Shelldrake, the sky starts to cry. About five miles up 23, the rain comes harder and then turns to hail. When it bounces off the windshield like Superballs and the windshield wipers make this whining sound, we pull beneath an overpass. Soon our breath clouds up the windshield and windows, and we can't tell if the storm's letting up or getting worse or if any other cars are going for it. Then Jake cracks his window and moves toward me, burying his head in the crook of my neck and cupping my breasts.

"So this is Paradise," he whispers, but it isn't, and I bite my bottom lip and try not to scratch his back as his hands slide over my ribs and belly and stroke between my legs.

It's not till a red livestock truck parks in front of us and dims its lights that I pull away, let out my breath. "I can't. It's that ..."

"Damn truck," Jake says, sliding away from me, and I lean over and kiss his cheek. I'm glad he's stopped but sad to feel so relieved. For a minute, I think about telling him about Don, about what he did. But then Jake starts up the Catalina and puts it in drive, and we're plowing through the storm again.

Some five miles north of Paradise, the storm ends and the signs for Shelldrake Lake begin. There's a different type of sign in front of Aunt Pauline and Don's lakefront log cabin: "For sale. Palazzolo Properties,

Inc." Behind the sign, Don's bent over an oval flower garden, hands digging into the dirt. He straightens when we pull alongside the aluminum garage where he used to hide his porno mags and dirty books—the garage where it happened. Then he limps our way. I want to hide, but Jake's already opening the passenger door and Don's already leaning on the fender, a bunch of red salvia dangling from his left hand.

"For your Aunt Pauline," he says, raising the salvia in the air. "Gonna frost tonight."

"Uncle Don, this is my friend Jake," I say, remembering the vise-like grip of his hands on my arms, my legs. As Jake shakes Don's free hand I wince: I just called him "Uncle," something I swore I'd never do.

I watch Don help Jake with our bags, trying not to stare at the beer belly hanging over his eagle-shaped brass belt buckle, at the kinky gray hairs growing out of his nose and ears. It makes me sick, that I'd ever let him touch me. But then I remember what Oprah said—that it wasn't my fault.

"Pauline, look who's here," Don shouts, ushering us through the cabin door. "Pauline? It's Cassie and her friend." He drops the salvia on the gray formica snack bar and motions toward the red vinyl barstools. "Sit right here—I'll get her."

Jake sits on the closest barstool while I scope the room. The furniture's about the same, only older, but the photographs on the mantle have all been changed. In place of those old photos of my mother, Aunt Pauline's little sister, are photos of me: me and my girlfriend Tammy at Pictured Rocks; me and Don at Taquamenon Falls; me, Don, and Aunt Pauline at Whitefish Point. I get the shivers just looking at them, wondering whether Aunt Pauline or Don put them there.

"Here she is," Don says, leading a shriveled and shrunken Aunt Pauline toward us.

I inch toward her and kiss her cheek, amazed that Aunt Pauline's come to this: a phantom of the gym teacher who raised me after my mother split.

"I dreamt you were making angels in the snow last night," she says, grasping my shoulders with trembling fish-bone hands and bringing her face close to mine. "I dreamt you were dancing in a long white dress and had wings instead of legs."

I freeze for a second. I've stripped in a long white dress—a see-through one with matching panties.

"Cassie," Jake says, rising.

"Aunt Pauline, this is Jake," I tell her, squeezing her hand. But I'm not sure she even recognizes me, and I'm real sure she won't remember Jake come morning.

"Alzheimer's," Don mumbles, shaking his head from side to side before reaching for the salvia. "More flowers for the lady," he tells Aunt Pauline, holding them in front of her nose before dropping them in a cut-glass vase on top of the microwave.

I feel this little flash of guilt—Don's being awfully nice to Aunt Pauline—before deciding it's just an act.

"They're real pretty, Aunt Pauline," I say, moving closer to the microwave. No water, of course, just a vase of wilting salvia.

✷

Later that night, after we eat carryout almond chicken and almond cookies and watch the *$20,000 Pyramid*, I try to talk to Aunt Pauline about old times. But the only old times she remembers are way before my time, back when she and Don swapped high-school photos and my mother wore her hair in pigtails.

"Anybody for a game of poker?" Don asks awhile later, but he's not looking at anybody, he's looking at me.

I wince, feeling a flush of shame flood my face. I've been readying for this for years, the chance to beat him at his own game, but I'm still not ready.

"Something quick, like jack pots," he adds. "Good way to kill time."

I suck in my breath. "Not jack pots. Seven-card stud ... you know, where the cards are on the table."

"Okay by me," Jake says, though he's got the luck of the Polish when it comes to cards.

Don hands me a tattered deck. "Your deal."

I grab the cards, careful to keep my fingers and eyes away from his, then deal them fast, like a pro.

"Shit," Jake says, and I can't blame him: ten of diamonds, jack of spades, king of hearts, and two red aces up, and knowing his luck, God knows what's buried.

I've got one great hand. A royal flush. I play it cool, frowning at the ten, queen, king, and ace of hearts that are face up on the folding table. Don's got three of a kind showing and guts when it comes to poker. He falls for my bluff, like I figured he would, and his eyes go marble when he sees my family in red. He sees red three more times, too, but we're not playing for money. Not yet.

"One more time, Cassie," he begs, handing me the cards.

"No," I say, refusing to take them. "I'm going to bed."

"Separate rooms, huh?" Jake asks.

"Aunt Pauline's like my mom," I answer, glad for the excuse. "I wouldn't feel right."

✷

I toss and turn from 10:00 untill 4:30, then wake up for good at 5:30. I put on my yellow terrycloth bathrobe and tiptoe toward the kitchen. But someone's there before me, someone else who can't sleep.

"Have a seat," Don says, raising his coffee cup and patting the barstool next to his.

I lean on the snackbar instead and stare at a cigarette burn in the pebbled formica—a burn I put there when I was twelve—then up at Don. "I don't think so," I say finally, voice low but clear, like when I laid down the royal flush.

Don rubs the corners of his eyes. "She saw another angel. A black one this time. Said it was singing 'Somewhere Over the Rainbow,' her favorite song."

I wonder about this for a minute, wonder if Aunt Pauline seeing angels, black or white, singing or dancing, is or isn't a good sign. "Great," I say, trying to open the pine cupboard above the garbage disposal, where the cups and glasses used to be, before noticing the lock.

"Meds and cleaning stuff," Don says. "She'll eat and drink anything. Drano, dish detergent, packages of laxatives."

"Drano?" I shake my head and reach for the "Get Well Soon" coffee cup on top of the microwave, left arm brushing against the vase of salvia. I peer closer, not quite believing it's half full of water—or that Don's taking such good care of Aunt Pauline.

Don gestures toward the coffeepot. "Help yourself."

I pour half a cup of coffee and sip it. "Like you did?"

"How's that?" Don asks, yawning.

I can't speak. I've been acting this out for months, and I can't speak. I want to run, to leave Shelldrake Lake here and now, with or without Jake, and go someplace safe, like Alaska. "Aunt Pauline still sleeping?" I ask instead.

"Who knows? Morning, noon, night—all the same to her."

I see another chance. "She's never been what I'd call observant. Take you, for instance."

"Me?"

"Maybe she just didn't want to see it. What you did."

"What I did?"

He's not going to make it easy. "Cute cup," I say, backing off. I trace the picture on the cup, a tan teddy bear holding a cluster of red and blue balloons.

"Got it at the hospital. Cost five big ones."

I can't believe he said that. I take a deep breath and put on my best poker face. "Five bucks? That's all?" But there's a pulse pounding in my head.

Don shrugs.

"I'm upping the ante, Don. Throw in the cup and a couple thousand bucks and I won't tell the world you're a child molester. What a deal."

"What?"

He said it casually, but his eyes looked glazed, like when I won three games straight. "You heard me."

"Unless you got proof, it's your word against mine," he says, staring me down.

I clench the "Get Well Soon" cup, afraid I might throw it.

"Donny?" Aunt Pauline hobbles into the room, leans against the lightswitch on the near wall.

"Oh, God," I whisper, because the lightswitch and the wall look cold, and because Aunt Pauline's not wearing any clothes. I can't help but stare: Her boobs sag like wet teabags and her crotch is caked with baby powder.

"Aahh, honey. . ." Don rises and slides out of his green velour bathrobe, throwing it over Aunt Pauline's shoulders and wrapping it around her like a coat. The yellow PJ's he's wearing beneath the robe are threadbare and his fat stretches them out, like pork sausage in a link casing.

"I don't have any clothes," Aunt Pauline whispers loud enough for me to hear.

Don squeezes her hand. "Come on, honey. You've got bushels of clothes. Let's go put some on."

I stand stone still as Don leads Aunt Pauline out of the room. He stripped my clothes off time after time. And now he's putting Aunt Pauline's back on. I walk to the hearth and sit down, gripping the coffee cup and trying not to cry.

Don walks back into the room a few minutes later. "Two-thousand bucks for the facts of life? Isn't that a bit much?"

I throw the cup, and the hurt I've slept with for the past nineteen years, at his head. The cup whizzes past him and bounces off the blue-and-white Currier & Ives plate I sent Aunt Pauline the Christmas before last, chipping the rim.

"Whoa, there," Don says, staring at the shards of china on the kitchen floor.

The hurt bounces off Don and back onto me. "You . . ." I try to speak, but it comes out a squeak. "You ruined my life. The stuff you made me do. . ."

"You've got legs. You could have walked."

"Are you saying I *liked* it?"

"Sure you did. Still do. What else you doing with that guy?"

I can't believe it, but Don actually sounds sincere. Dumb, but sincere. "I was just a kid then. I'm a woman now. There's a difference."

"You seemed woman enough to me. And you were always hanging around, like you wanted loving."

"I did want loving," I tell him, eyes stinging. "But not that kind. Not that kind at all. And where was I supposed to go?"

"Besides," he says, as if trying to change the subject, "Pauline and I don't have $2,000."

"But you will. You will when you sell this place."

"Take my money and you take your Aunt Pauline's." Don pauses, pours himself another cup of coffee. "She's gonna need it if something happens to me. Unless *you're* planning on taking care of her."

I can't believe he's bringing Aunt Pauline into this. I stare at him, wishing I'd never come, wishing I was back tracking sunbeams at Taquamenon or dancing at the Silver Scissors.

"You can't blame a guy for trying," he pleads.

I stand up, turn my back on Don, and stare at the mantle. The photo of Don, Aunt Pauline, and me at Whitefish Point stares back. Lake Superior whitecaps rage behind us, thrusting three feet into the air, and pine boughs frame our faces. I bite my lower lip, wondering if Hiawatha ever paddled his canoe through such nasty waters, and if pine boughs start or stop a fire. "I could tell the guys in that CB club of yours. Might give them something worth talking about. Or what's left of the family."

"You wouldn't do that, honey," Don says. "You don't have it in you to do that."

"And I could compare notes with Cousin Linda. Did she want loving, too?" The cards are on the table. "Think about that," I say, moving toward the hallway. When I reach it I do a half-turn and glance back, surprised to see that Don looks beat. The cards are on the table, and the ante's mine. But I still feel bad.

⁕

Five hours later, I slide my suitcase into the Catalina's back seat. There's an IGA grocery bag next to it that wasn't there when we arrived. I can't believe what's in the bag: a walnut cuckoo clock with gingerbread trim, the same cuckoo clock that once hung on Aunt Pauline's bedroom wall. I used to run to that clock at least a dozen times a day, waiting to see the cuckoo's orange beak peek out and hear its chipper song.

How I loved Aunt Pauline's cuckoo! But not enough to take it from her. And not in place of my $2,000.

I pull the grocery bag out of the car and march back into the cabin with it. "I don't want this," I say, placing it on the snackbar in front of Don while a puzzled Jake looks on.

Aunt Pauline sits on the far barstool, shoulders slumped forward, picking at a piece of whole-wheat toast.

"What in the hell you talking about?" Don asks.

"Just forget it, okay? I don't want your money; I don't want a God-damned thing from you."

"Cuckoo, cuckoo," Aunt Pauline says, bending even more forward and peering into the bag.

"Cuckoo?" Don reaches into the bag and removes the clock.

"It's Aunt Pauline's cuckoo clock," I tell Jake, who's looking at the three of us like we're as cuckoo as the clock.

"Cuckoo, cuckoo," Aunt Pauline says again, trying to rise. "Cassie loves the cuckoo."

Don looks at me and winks. "She must want you to have it," he says, putting the clock back into the bag and handing it to me.

"Yeah," I whisper, holding the bag in my left arm and Aunt Pauline's fragile body in my right. "Yeah, I've always loved the cuckoo." I look into Aunt Pauline's gray eyes but she's gone again, gone to a place where white angels dance and black angels sing and there's nothing in between.

Don walks us to the car while Aunt Pauline watches from the front window.

"You'd better take good care of her," I tell him as Jake starts up the car. "Really good care of her."

"Always do."

"I do have proof," I whisper, leaning against the passenger door and pulling two shoddy paperbacks out of my purse. "Books you put in my suitcase the last time I was here. Books with your name in them. *Ticket to Paradise* and *The Joy Ride*. And don't forget Cousin Linda." I smile sweetly as Don's face turns this shocking shade of pink, like the velour stretch pants I wore on Christmas Eve, then slip the books back in my purse.

The wild card, if I ever have to use it.

"Ready, Cassie Pants?" Jake asks, opening the door and patting my ass.

"No," I say, pushing his hand away. "But drive anyway. And don't call me that. Don't ever call me that again."

About the Writers

Margo LaGattuta, editor, is a poet with four published books: *Embracing the Fall* (Plain View Press), *The Dream Givers* (Lake Shore Publishing), *No Edge Lines* (Earhart Press) and *Diversion Road* (State Street Press). She has an MFA from Vermont College, teaches writing at Oakland Community College and hosts a weekly radio interview program. Her poems and essays have appeared in many literary magazines and presses.

Nancy J. Henderson received her MA in Creative Writing from Antioch University in 1994. She has published poems in literary journals and worked as an editor for a trade publication. She is single and lives in Michigan, but spends as much time as she can in the southwest mountains and desert. She is also an avid country western dancer and horseback rider.

Mary Ann Wehler has been a daughter, friend, wife, mother, teacher and grandmother. In her sixties, she has become a writer.

Aline Soules has published in *The MacGuffin, Peninsula Poets, Alura Quarterly, Tandava, The Detroit Magazine* and *The Northville Record.* Her background includes a BA (Honors), an MA, an MSLS and creative writing courses at the Iowa Summer Writing Festaval.

Susan Knoppow is a writer and trainer, currently working toward a Master of Fine Arts degree in Writing at Vermont College. Her poems, essays and articles have appeared in numerous publications.

Pearl Kastran Ahnen, a former newspaper editor and journalist, made the transition to fiction several years ago. Her fiction and poetry have been published in literary journals, her plays staged in theaters. In 1992, she won the Michigan Livingston County Arts Council Award in Literary Arts for Fiction.

Gerry Tamm, in her former life, taught communications to college students. Now she follows her own muse. Her work has appeared in such diverse places as *The Wall Street Journal* and *Highlights for Children*. She is active in the Poetry Society of Michigan and edited their latest anthology, *Heart Songs*.

Sandy Gerling lives not twenty miles from where she was born and raised in Rochester, Michigan. She holds degrees as a registered nurse, which she practiced for ten years, and a commercial artist. She has been published in *Sun* magazine. She now divides her time between painting, writing, and her family of husband and two children.

Vivian DeGain earned her BA in Communication Arts (journalism) from the University of Michigan in 1992. A wife and a mother of three, she works as a staff writer for *The Rochester Clarion* and has published as a free-lance writer, poet and editor.

Nancy Ryan is a free-lance writer and an adjunct instructor at Oakland Community College. A member of the Oakland Writer's Group, Michigan Playwrights and a salon of fellow writers, she has gleaned much and owes much. She is co-author of *The Customer-Driven Company*, *The Process-Driven Business* and *Buttonbush*. Her poetry and fiction have appeared in *Elan*, *Getting the Knack* and *The MacGuffin*.

Variations on the Ordinary is published in a first edition of 2000 copies the first 400 of which are signed and numbered.